HEARING THE VOICE OF GOD

HEARING THE VOICE OF God

KAREN COFFEY

TATE PUBLISHING *& Enterprises*

Published in the United States of America

ISBN: 1–5988652–4–2
06.09.06

Hearing the Voice of God

by Karen Coffey

ACKNOWLEDGMENTS

*A*S I PREPARE TO WRITE this thank you and acknowledgement to all the people that have made a difference in my life, I'm struck by my sudden want to include everyone I've met, everyone I've had the pleasure of interacting with. It's because of every person I've met that I have become who I am and I've received so many gifts from them all, seen and unseen, but I know that there are those chosen few, chosen by our long-standing agreements with one another, even before we were born, that said, "I will see you and the beauty that you are, no matter what you choose to show me on the outside of yourself, I **will** see you; beauty and light, and child of God."

God, and all that that entails, I want to thank first. Without the beautiful softness of his touch every day I could never have written these words. He continues to believe in me and my abilities when I fail to believe in myself. To Mike, whose love and support has seen me through my darkest hours, whose wit and unfathomable talent never ceases to amaze me. To my dear friend Meredith who had the courage to love me and pray with me that night before God spoke. To Cindy, how can I thank you enough. Your beauty and wisdom that answered and continues to answer my every question about God and life; you are my dearest friend and I love you. To my son, Christopher, who never fails to see the light inside of me.

God has given me so much support in my life over

the past three years to accomplish the mission he and I set myself upon. One in particular I want to thank is Neale Donald Walsch for always holding the light and the vision for all of us and allowing me to share in that vision for two years now. My 25 brothers and sisters of Ashland that will always live deeply in my heart forever, you know who you are, thanks and thanks again. To Rachael, Estera, Maria, and John, you have changed my life completely and I am forever grateful!

With deep gratitude I thank my mother and father who raised me with great love and intention of a better way of life. I thank my Grandmother Lane for all the late night readings of the Bible and to the mountains of east Tennessee where I first felt the hand of God, I say thank you. What an incredible ride it has been . . . thank you all!

PREFACE

*T*HE FUTURE HOLDS SUCH GREAT promise for us all as we become closer, more connected, to our beautiful source, our God. We all must learn how to listen carefully to God and our inner voice. It is a new day for which we are dawning. A day in which every man and woman will learn to have a very personal and close relationship with God. This God is the same God Almighty, Father in heaven, Allah and Father, Mother God that we all pray to. There is no difference. There is only One. Because there are so many divisions on the matter of truth it is imperative that each person achieve that greater connection with God and self. It is more than a brief "walking in the clouds" kind of connection to God; it is a connection that you never have to depart from. It is a complete clarity of mission and purpose that can only be given to us daily through God and our connection with him. Once this door is opened wide, the connection to Source never has to leave and we can access it at any moment. It is our comforter, our communicator, and the light that shines before us when we are in darkness.

I never thought this possible until God began writing these letters. He showed me that our birthright is to live in a natural state of confidence, peace, and love for one another. Confidence, peace, and love were not natural states of being for me. I thank God, the angels and all my guides and teachers for this miracle in my life and I want with all my heart for us all to receive the miracle, the gift of constant Christ consciousness, so that we can live with complete clarity and purpose, always staying in the light, connected at all times and truly bringing heaven on earth to all people.

In God's love. . . .

*K*AREN

INTRODUCTION

*T*HERE ARE AND HAVE BEEN so many before me that have taken dictation, so to speak, from a much higher presence than they themselves, and of themselves, could have ever attained. I of myself could never have written the words and messages that follow. My walk through life has been no more significant than most people. It's been three years since this experience began and I am still listening to God. The voice changed over time as I became busier again and life took on some normalcy. The biggest question I always get is how did you know if was the voice of God speaking to you. Well, I don't propose to know a lot of things, but I will say, when the voice of God speaks to you, you know it; there is no mistaking it. Like I said, the voice has changed over time, not as loud and booming as that first day, but God knew how to get my attention and after all it took three times even then of him gently but persistently saying, "Go write something down."

I feel as though I owe you, the reader, some history into my life and experiences and I guess you could easily put the book down now, because I have never thought my life was anything significant. I've always thought I was different and maybe even a bit special, but I'd have never let you know it; that would be bragging or "showing out" my grandmother would say. Why, why, why is it we don't allow ourselves to shine, to really be ourselves out in the world? I am more irritated with myself than anything, because after 40 years of life on earth I'm just now getting it. Just now realizing how special each one of us is and that every individual on earth has something special about them that they bring the planet. I won't go about preaching just yet, I'll save that for later, but back to my story . . . and it is a story, you know, all of it made up from our own beliefs and perceptions. Anyway . . .

It's really one of those Mayberry, USA, kind of beginnings. I had deep auburn hair and freckles growing up, which never makes you extremely popular in school. It's almost as if life is saying your doomed before you even open your mouth. Oh, how I wanted to be blonde! Add to that a little chubbiness and the fact I was the tallest person in school and you get the picture; I was sunk when it came to dating and fitting in.

I have to laugh every time I hear the saying "yeah, but she's got a great personality." That was me all over! I could have the whole crowd in stitches, laughing about just real-life, embarrassing stuff. I believe one of my talents growing up was just being observant of other people and how they felt at any given time and then making them laugh about it whether it was sad, embarrassing or even irritating. I've never been one to remember jokes so I never told any. Even now my husband can tell me the same joke over and over again, as long as there are a few years in between, and I still don't remember them. I had to stick with real-life situations.

Anyway, back to my great personality and natural good looks . . . I found myself overcompensating with my personality. I was not really shy, just insecure about myself because I wasn't all of those things I thought a girl should be. Cute, petite, even lady-like to name a few. I enjoyed for the most part being alone. I wasn't introverted oddly enough; I was extremely outgoing and social. I would later find out that it was because in order for me to be "ON" a lot, I need to be "OFF" even more.

A perfect example of this came two years ago when I bought the cutest little cabin in the mountains as a weekend getaway home for our family and ended up moving there full time. Situated in a valley surrounded by mountains on about four acres of beautiful land, it was an hour and a half to the closest Mall. When I say I was alone, I mean alone. Your hand wouldn't show up in front of you on a moonless night, but the stars sure would.

In those times when I'm alone and can get silent, that is when I most easily hear the voice of God. Not the voice of ego, not the world talking at me, but the gentle voice of one who knows and loves me like no one else can. It's sometimes difficult for those close to me to understand why I want to be alone so much of the time, without taking it personal, but they have come to understand why. God is why! All of my life, more than anything in my life, I have always wanted to know God intimately.

I was "born again" in the Baptist church when I was twelve. My father was a deacon and my mother taught Sunday school. We graced the doors of that little church morning, noon and night it seemed as a little girl, and not once can I remember feeling the love of God. Oh, I can remember a lot of other feelings, like fear that I would anger God and guilt over some of the thoughts I was having, but never love. I remember extreme boredom and thinking to myself if God is alive, and I've been told he is, where do I find him? I never once blamed the pastor or the elders in the church. In some way I knew they were trying to live good lives and living them the only way they knew how, but I also knew there was something more we weren't getting. I didn't realize at the time it was Holy Spirit I was missing. Holy Spirit just wasn't showing up for some reason and at age eighteen I began my quest to find and know God.

So what did I do but join the biggest Baptist church within a 100-mile radius of where I lived. I knew they must know God and the first thing the elders did was put me on the witnessing team. You know what that is—it's when you go door to door evangelizing about Jesus Christ to all the people that are going to hell. Okay, I thought I could do that. I might be pretty good at preaching to the back sliding masses . . . until one day, we showed up at a girl's house I had known in high school. She and her family were by far the nicest, non-judgmental people I had ever met in my life. You want to talk about SWEET! Lisa was sweet. She was always full of love for other people.

She let us in and my team of Christian experts and I sat in her living room to began explaining why each and every soul on earth needs to accept Jesus Christ as their personal lord and savior or they will be sent to hell and eternal damnation. Now I was not saying a word because I knew Lisa personally, so I let the older folks do the talking. It wasn't thirty minutes into the presentation when I knew somewhere in my heart that Lisa wasn't going to hell, and neither was her family. If anybody in that house was going to hell it would probably be me for spreading such bologna. Jesus said, "None can get to the father but by me," which in Aramaic meant I am your example, I am your way shower. None can get to the Father but by my example. I have come to show you how to have the relationship I have with the Father, just do as I do and it will be done. Greater things than this will you do! I call this day my day of remembering. I remembered "our" divinity. I knew that Jesus was my brother, my Christed teacher and yes, even the son of God. He was indeed one with the Father as we will also one day be. This was just a knowing inside of me and I never went back to the witnessing team. I did continue with Bible studies and questioned every statement the poor teacher would make. I decided it would be better for everyone if I bowed out of these studies as I looked for another church. Nothing ever felt quite right, so I stopped searching.

Months later on a Sunday morning as I was getting ready to visit my mother, I heard the words "be as Paul was" in a very loud and distinct voice. I knew I was home alone, the TV wasn't on, and forgive my boldness, but I was in the shower. All I was hearing was the water above my head. Needless to say it shocked the heck out of me and I told everybody I knew. They all had the same response . . . hmmph! Everyone was sort of complacent about it, not quite sure what to think. I didn't hear it again for a long time, and surely never forgot it either. It was not a message I acted on or even knew how to act on. I remember opening the Bible to learn a little more about Paul thinking that would in some way give me a clue as to what to do, but nothing came to me and I let it go from my mind.

Life was very normal for me, whatever that means, for many years. What I mean by normal is getting a job, then a career, then social climbing, and then getting married, having children and then waking up and saying, "Oh my God, what have I done with my life?" Now, I am in no way insinuating that everyone's life is this way, but I'll be darned if that's not how many of them turned out. Over the years I lost my chubbiness and highlighted my hair, so dating got better and much more frequent, thank God. In 1990 I moved to Atlanta, Georgia, and it wasn't too much longer that I met my husband. Interestingly enough, it was the moment I gave up on men that I met him. He was my next-door neighbor.

It was a whirlwind romance and I want to say I couldn't believe it when the stories the old ladies had told me came true. They would say things like, "You will feel it with the first kiss," or, "You'll just know it in your bones." What poppycock, I thought, until it happened to me. We were married within 7 months. What the old ladies didn't tell me was that bliss is sometimes short lived. What truly made the difference in our relationship was my husband . . . his love and sincere commitment to our marriage. I would like to say it was me, but it wasn't. I was young and immature and wouldn't have known true commitment if it had hit me. I desperately wanted to be a good wife, but I discovered, and relationships will do this to you, that I was an angry, insecure, emotionally unstable woman. I don't know how Mike put up with me the first two years of our marriage, but I thank God he did, because his sticking it out with me helped to change and shape me into a beautiful woman who loves every person she meets and above all, loves herself.

You see, I didn't like myself and I didn't even know it, until Mike loved me and loved me and loved me some more and taught me I had no one to blame for my misery. I'd push him away and push him away and he wouldn't leave me. I'd yell, I'd get mad, I'd even throw things sometimes. I just kept testing him, maybe you are familiar with how some of us do that. I guess we just have to make sure one more time. That is just crazy! That's crazy thinking and crazy behavior. I got better, though. I got help and let me strongly urge anyone who might be acting like that to get some help. For me it took a psychiatrist that told me I needed to go to a 12-step program and get my thinking straightened out. What in the world . . ."But, Doctor, I don't drink." He said, "I don't care, you need a power that is greater than yourself to heal you, and I'm not it." It was wake-up time and grow-up time and I hated every minute of it. I've never fought anything so hard in all my life. It's as if I would've rather thrown up than let go of "control," so to speak. My behaviors and beliefs that were so precious to me, were killing me, literally. I was on death's doorstep because I could not control my thinking or life and situations around me.

I promised when I began this book I would be completely transparent and I will be. I began going to AA meetings once a week. That's Alcoholics Anonymous. They would only let me into the open speakers meetings and the blue book study. The blue book for those who don't know was written by a man fondly called Bill W. It is one of the greatest divinely inspired books of our time and if you've never read it please do. It has saved the lives of millions. Please know that you don't have to be an alcoholic, as I quickly learned, to have your life changed by this book and the AA program. So I went to those meetings and my life began to change and people noticed. I began forgiving everyone in my life, even if I thought they might have even remotely hurt my feelings. You see, the forgiving was for me, not them. By my letting the hurt go, whether real or imagined, I was able to be stronger and move forward in my life with integrity, because I had done the right thing. Every step of it was done with God's help, every step. As AA teaches you that you cannot do it alone, you must hand it over to a power greater than yourself, and I did, and guess what . . . the bliss came back. It came back in my marriage and my life.

Mike and I eventually found a church in our area that we liked and life was good. So good in fact we had a baby, a boy we named Christopher. Ten toes and ten little fingers and off to the races we went, moving from Atlanta to Tennessee, Ohio, back to Georgia for two months and then Florida and back again to Georgia. Whew! See what I mean? Raising kid(s) and climbing those ladders will eat up the time we have here on earth in a heartbeat. It's not until the heartbeat runs out or starts aching that we realize there is something more important about our lives. In my case my heartbeat started hurting and I guess that's fortunate because if it had run out, I'd be dead.

Climbing ladders had brought me to a place in life where I worked about 60 hours a week and I was burned out at my job. I was doing very well financially, winning all kinds of awards, but I was starting to get miserable . . . again. On second thought I wasn't starting to, I *was* miserable. Everything on the relationship front was going well this time; it was just the rest of life I couldn't stand. Okay, really only work, but that consumed the rest of my life so it felt like everything in my life stunk. I had indeed lost my balance and the universe was kind enough to let me know it early on by giving me severe chest pains. I think back on it now and it's so interesting that my chest pains began in church. Hmmmm. God, are you trying to tell me something? I was only 37 years old at this time so

I couldn't be having a heart attack, could I? I blamed it on the new spirit-filled church we had begun going to. By spirit filled I mean filled with the Spirit of God, which is Holy Spirit. And that Spirit began to move in me.

I left church immediately and went to the hospital to be checked. They did every test they could think of and couldn't find a thing wrong with me. I went home exhausted and out of breath. I couldn't even go up one flight of stairs without stopping and sitting down.

Four days went by and I was thoroughly depressed. A friend called that week to see how my condition was, I began to cry telling her, "I am so miserable physically and emotionally and there is nothing wrong with my life."

Three days after our conversation my friend called again and said, "I have been given a message from God and I want to come pray with you tonight." Well, there has never been a time in my life when I wanted to hear a "message from God" from one of my friends . . . but this was not like any other time in my life. It was different and I was desperate.

"Great, what time?" I heard myself say.

She came and we prayed that night with my husband watching. I desperately wanted something big to happen, something dramatic, but nothing came except tears as I realized how low I had become. Here I was, my best friend was praying over me in the living room as my husband watched. If there was an ounce of pride left in my body, it was gone at this moment. As she prayed that night, the softest, sweetest voice came through in a language I had never heard. It was beautiful even though I had no idea what she was saying. Up until this point in my life I had never heard a person speak in tongues. It was beautiful and touching.

She left that night and I felt no different. There had been no boom, no voices from the heavens, nothing dramatic.

The next day my son went off to summer camp and my husband went off to work. I was sitting alone, chest hurting, sitting in that same living room as the night before and I started praying to a God I had known in childhood. I prayed to that God Almighty, Father in heaven, that I had grown up with. I prayed out loud, or should I say yelled out loud, my prayer. I was asking—okay, yelling—for the Holy Spirit to come to me and strike out any negative, evil or unclean thing that might have attached itself to me. This prayer was so completely foreign to me, so different from what I had become used to that it scared me, but I prayed it anyway. I figured God knew what I meant.

I began to yell louder and cry harder. I wanted my misery to be gone more that anything in this world. I asked that Holy Spirit would fill the void in my life and cleanse every part of my body. In the midst of this praying something interrupted me, sort of like station identification, right in the middle of my program.

I feel I must digress a little bit at this point because I feel a certain event that happened a few weeks earlier is very important to explain how Spirit was moving in me.

Two weeks prior to this time of my chest hurting, Mike, Christopher and I went to Italy on vacation. Our first stop was Venice and the second night we are there I was awakened in the middle of the night so cold that I was shaking violently. It was June in Venice and

72 degrees outside with no air conditioning in the room. Mike had to wrap me with numerous blankets and rub me down before the shaking would subside. When my teeth stopped chattering enough to speak I told Mike, "I don't know what that was, but it was big." What I meant was I have no idea how to explain it, but I knew that was an important experience.

Now here is another question. How did I know my body temperature didn't just drop? Well, I don't know except I can only relay to you what was *felt*, which is so much more important than our logical explanations for it. I will never try to convince anyone of my experience, but when you hear, touch, or feel God, you absolutely know it. there is no denying it. I now know that was the beginning of my baptism in Spirit so to speak. It was around me, in me and through me. Every cell and muscle in my body was touched by it, raising a vibration in me to allow me to hear the messages I was about to hear in just a few short weeks.

Back at home . . . two weeks later . . .

The loudest, strongest voice I'd ever heard said, "Go Write." I had no idea what it was and ignored it, promptly getting back to praying, but then it came again. "Go Write." I was sure I was about to have a breakthrough in my prayer and this "voice" was annoying me, so once again I ignored it. The third time the interruption came I decided I better listen. It obviously had something more important to tell me than what I was saying. (Isn't that ironic.)

Always keeping an old notebook on my nightstand, I picked it up, put pen to paper and wrote these few lines:

Of God I seek in days gone past
Yearning for to be by his side

And then a soft voice answered:

Love me thy beautiful spirit
Your days are long before we meet again
Thine heart is pure, full of forgiveness and truth
Let not your footsteps be altered or ignored
Glory to God this day

I knew clearly and without a doubt that I had not written those words. Page after page came forth in three-and four-word increments. I never knew how a sentence would end or what would be next. The voice came to me daily with word upon word and I wrote for hours without ceasing at times. It was never an out-of-body experience or even a trance-like state. It was always as if a higher power was placing the words and sentences into my mind, gently, but very strongly.

I heard theses messages at first and then I began seeing visions in my mind. It was either images and things that had happened long in the past or visions of things that hadn't occurred yet. I didn't see like this all the time, but I found the more I heard and wrote the messages that Spirit was giving me, the more connected with all kinds of information I would be. I could hear and see Mike's deceased father come through and want to talk with him, I'd see all kinds of people who had been killed. They would come down my halls at night just to talk or show me something that had happened to them because they knew I could hear and see them. Information such as dates and times that events would happen would come to me even without asking, but my main focus was always on God and his messages.

Am I psychic? I've never cared for the word psychic. There have been so many that have had bad experiences with those who are psychic, but don't take it to a higher level or a higher vibration of understanding. I believe, as with everything, there are many levels of understanding and consciousness. I like to think I'm just connected at a high level.

You know Jesus said to his disciples after he ascended into heaven that by the power of the Holy Spirit in them and about them, they would be able to connect with God. They would be gifted with speaking in languages they themselves did not know. Some would have the gift of discernment and others the gift of prophecy, wisdom and knowledge. This channel that I have become is only using the gift of knowledge and prophecy that has been given me by God (Acts 2:17).

All have the ability to listen and hear God, but not all will. Even though we all have the ability to speak in tongues foreign to us, not all will. And here is why . . . the Spirit needs a vehicle that is humble, trusting and faithful in God alone. If you speak to anyone who has the Spirit of God in their lives in full measure it is because before having their "spiritual experience" they most times experienced a lot of personal pain. The dark night of the soul once again. These dark nights can come numerous times in your life, every one created to propel you forward and upward to a higher understanding of yourself, of life and of God.

Does this mean if you don't have one of these gifts you're not living right or you're not as good as someone who does? Absolutely not! You are right where you're meant to be for your spiritual growth and evolution. Here is the great news: We're living in a time where the veil that separates heaven from earth is thinning. This means more and more people are hearing, feeling, seeing things of the Spirit. They are receiving their gifts and you will continue to see this around every corner. We are lifting our planet higher and higher each day by connecting to our God, our Source, by being the light in our homes and communities, by continuously holding loving thoughts about ourselves and others instead of allowing negative thoughts and situations to run away with our minds.

What an exciting time we live in. We are all moving higher to a time of our own selves being Christed and remembering our oneness with God.

To say incredible things began happening in my life is an understatement. I was able to leave work and stay at home writing full time, at least for the year it took to write these messages. My husband's position took off, which allowed me to do this comfortably. Was it coincidence or was it aligning with God and the universe? I like to think that when we give ourselves permission, when we allow ourselves to be a channel of divine inspiration, the universe and the powers that be align to support us in our every desire. Let me go off on a tangent, just for a moment indulge me.

Where did we ever get the idea God wanted us to be poor? Are we that unworthy? One of the lessons I really got during this time of writing was that God is the Source of all things. My source would not be my job, nor my husband's job, but God. There were numerous times, too many to include here, where for no apparent reason other than an extreme faith in God, I was blessed abundantly beyond my comprehension. $55,000 one July, $6,000 one December, our house selling without even putting it on the market when every house around us was taking up to a year to sell?

But the biggest blessing of all, the one that was so obviously God, was when we went on vacation to Florida. We stayed in a friend's condo for a week for $100, and while I was there, writing on the beach one morning, God said, "Look for a property of your own here." My whole body said, "What!" I argued for quite a while. How will I ever tell Mike that God said we are to buy an ocean-front condo. I could just imagine his response. He has been so accepting of all this new information coming into our lives, but this I was sure would send him over the edge. Mikes was surprised when I told him this. We had many reservations, mainly revolving around not having the money, but we did it, we stepped out in faith and called a realtor. We found the perfect two bedroom, two bath ocean-front ninth floor condo and we put a contract on it. Well, putting a contract and actually getting the money together to buy it are two different things.

The area custom was to put 10% down. That was $30,000 and we only had $15,000. I prayed and meditated and God spoke once again and said, "You have $16,000 in an IRA that hasn't moved since the internet bust in the late 90's. I am your source now and I will forever be your source, even in retirement. Take that money and I will make sure you are blessed." So we did!

It wasn't one week later I was crying to my minister about how I didn't have grocery money and how stupid of me to think I had heard God's voice tell me to buy an ocean-front condo. I told her I was sure it must have been my ego and my friend had one and I wanted one too. But I knew that wasn't it. I knew where my heart was. My heart was pure and so was my motive. I only want to do what Spirit tells me to do.

We got through it and money began to flow to us again. We closed on the condo and spent one of the best weeks of my life there, waking up to the sound of the ocean and the sunrises each day. Our friends and family used it and then . . . six months later . . . I heard the voice again regarding the condo. "Call your realtor in Florida and just see what's going on with prices; you need to sell it."

What! I was not pleased about this new plan, but Mike called and prices had skyrocketed to the tune of over 50%. We sold our perfect condo on the ocean in under two weeks for $160,000 more than what we had bought it for 6 months earlier. That's exactly ten times the amount we took out of the IRA that had been sitting there for five years.

Now I know what many will say. "God doesn't tell us when to play the lottery and what house to buy and doesn't this seem awfully materialistic for God to get involved in? And don't forget about capital gains tax because you didn't hold onto it for two years."

Come on, folks. Grow up! If God can bless us ten times over in six months time he can surely figure out how to pay taxes on the darn thing. God wants us to be abundantly blessed and he wants to be part of every decision in our lives, not just when we get stuck or are in need. God's will is for you to be happy, joyous, and prosperous. Why would he keep any information from us that would allow us to be any of those things? I choose to believe in a God that loves me fully and completely and that means he is my source in all things.

(Just as a footnote to this story, some of you remember the year three hurricanes hit Florida. We sold our condo in August and all three hurricanes hit Florida in September causing major damage to the lobbies of all the buildings in that area. I'm so glad we listened to the message that was given to us.)

After the messages were complete, and boy did I know when they were completed, they just stopped. I went back to work. You recall I did not like my job and how out of balance I was, so I went back to make peace, so to speak, so I could move on. Many times in our lives if we don't make peace with a situation we keep attracting it into our lives over and over again. We have to move through the pain of it and not just run away and hide. If we don't make peace, we are destined to repeat it again and again and I did not want to do that. I went back and I set up my schedule so that I left everyday at 1:00 in the afternoon, I only worked on weekends when absolutely necessary and refused to work with people who were unpleasant and stressed me out. I was ruthless in sticking with this agreement I had made to myself.

The result . . . I made exactly the same amount of money I had made the year before, but only worked until one o'clock everyday, only worked with people I enjoyed and I only worked 8 months that year. Hmmmm! Very interesting!

When I was done with that position, I could run to our mountain house and rest, which I did. I can't tell you what I did for that year, but I know it was stress free. We could never get anything done there. I tried to work from there, my husband tried to work from there, and every time we tried, we failed. The front porch sitting on the noisy creek would hypnotize us every time. I tried to write. I tried to teach. None of it ever got done. Friends would visit and say the same thing: "This is not a place for work, only for resting." So I gave up and just rested.

I feel it important to tell you I am so grateful every single day for all that has happened in the last few years, but there are still so many times when I doubt myself. The days are not always rosy. Fear creeps in regularly as I receive messages that tell me there is so much more to do. Life many times just gets in the way. I can look back and thank God for what he's shown me and done in my life, but when you're in it, I mean really in the middle of "it," I know it hurts and it's frustrating.

As you read through this collection of 135 letters, you will notice some of the type has been italicized. These are my personal prayers to God. They were my soul's cry at the time, much in the same way David cried out his Psalms of joy, gratitude and pain.

It is time for all of us in the world to begin receiving our own messages from God. In a world full of chaos it is time for us to receive our own peace. I am not the one who wrote these words, but God, a higher power, the Christ, who put each word on paper through me. I **know** all of us can do all things . . . and it is time. I am no more significant or closer to God than any one of you and this I know this with all my heart . . .

PART I

LETTER 1

Of God I seek in days gone past
Yearning for to be by his side.

Love me thy beautiful spirit
Your days are long before we
Meet again. Thine heart is pure
Full of forgiveness and truth.
Let not your footsteps be altered or ignored.
Glory to God this day

And then the many words that followed began in two or three word intervals . . .

THE WORDS I SPEAK ARE not my own but of my Father in heaven. Praise be to God for his love and understanding of our souls.

Love only me and not the world. It will only lead you away from me. Reflect upon the things I can give you, not what the world has to offer.

Keep your eyes on me always, lifting your heart and your head towards heaven, letting no one entice you. Look always for his love of God first.

Forlorned and alone are my people, yet I have never left them. Alas, you are my good servant . . . find them. Let them know of the heavenly riches they stand to inherit upon this earth . . . the love, the peace, and the joy available to them. I long for their return, to be in my presence.

In their moments of anguish, let them seek the light

of a thousand years. The light that continues to illumine their paths, yet they cannot see. Remind them to ask in fervent prayer for their every need, giving no thought as to how small or large the request. It is my love for you that makes this possible. Give yourself to me as I have given myself to you. That is the *only* sacrifice I desire.

You are my beloved children, full of rage and anger; not even realizing it is within you. Why do you think you act the ways you do in business and personal relationships? Long to be with me as I long to be with you. Lose yourself to the love of the Almighty Father not to the worldly behaviors that do not serve you.

Stop and recognize me, and ALL of who I am. I am all around you. Your sweetest, softest, most tender moments. I am the feeling of peace when you look across the water. I am the feeling of well being when you see the mountains. I am the infinite connection that carries you through to the other side of your being . . . The God side waiting to be found, touched and acknowledged.

Let it be brought forth into your everyday life. What are you hiding it from? My Son spoke the words that "the truth will set you free." The truth is "your" truth that will set "you" free. Do not ignore your own path to freedom. Counsel with me and ask what your truth is. Ask daily if need be. We will find a way, you and I, to communicate and you will know the peace, the peace that passes all understanding, and the knowing will lead you to your next step. Amen.

LETTER 2

PRAISE BE TO GOD!

Wherefore shall we begin to decipher the laws of God and how they collide with the laws of man? There is no one distinction that can be pointed out, but many. My good children, your faces are saddened with the misunderstanding of it all. Quiet your minds and listen to all that I have come to tell you.

Our world is here with you now and not so different. What we see is the same, but we see with purity. We wear no filters to distort the vibrant hues of life. We are so close to one another—my world and yours coexist. I reach out to touch you and you cannot see. Please open your eyes and your heart to those of us that surround you and love you with all our hearts. We are here only to help you and guide you to the side of yourself that lives fully without reservation. My Father in heaven seeks a oneness with all of his children, and especially those that fervently seek his companionship. He will never turn any man away, lest this man cannot find forgiveness of any kind in his heart.

My children, you must obey and adhere to this law of forgiveness. I want *all* of my children to understand that which keeps him from tasting the manna, feasting on life and thirsting for nothing. Praise and Glory to God, my children. There is nothing you have done which my father will not gladly forgive. And likewise, take this message to your family, your people, and strive, with the understand-ing of my faith, to forgive all who have wronged you. Even those you think you have no basis to hate, forgive them and yourself for your falsehood.

It is not a sin to believe in your greatness, with the knowledge that it is in co-existence with the Father. For-give and make peace with yourself and the many things you feel. Begin again! Begin again in the softness and security of my arms that hold you. Forgive your brothers and sisters. They are no different from you, living the only illusion they know to live. Pray for their awakening as well as your own. Knowing the path to your greatness is in God, working through you.

Halleluiah! My Joy burns immensely in my heart as I see my children coming home. The same love and joy will well up within you all as you see your brothers and sisters called home. Called home to serve. Called to work that is undone.

Gifted with the Spirit, the Christed ones will chal-lenge the worldly ways of doing all things. They will chal-lenge every thought, every fear, every common way of doing. Their light will be immense and will be recognized by all. Make way and open up your hearts and your homes to them. Love and support them, as many will not. They will lead the way these coming days. Many of you are the ones chosen. You will know. You will have the desire I have placed within your hearts. You will know the time to shout it from the mountaintops, as well as the time to whisper among friends. Stay with me in this time of greatness. The wheat will be sifted from the chaff. That does not mean the latter will be pushed aside, they are just as important in my father's eyes, but there will be a discernment, a reckoning if you will. Has your house been cleared? Ask for purity. Ask for light to show you anything that might be left to forgive, anything left unsaid, and anything that is unlike God in your heart. Ask to be shown and push nothing aside. If it is shown, it will need your attention. Light a candle and envision peace within your body and your life. Holding each area that came up in prayer, giving it to God the Father, seeing the situation peaceful and resolved. Let it float toward the heavens. Give it not another thought.

Be aware of negative thoughts that will naturally come into focus during this and many other prayer times. Follow me anyway. Follow me through this time of forgiveness to the time of love. I am the Night turned to Day. Hold me and I will not let go of you. I and my Father take over for you now. Step down and place your faith in the Three. Our love is overflowing for you. Prepare and make room for us in your life.

hatred in the world, but as we hold true to our purposes in life, those of hatred and belligerence will fade away.

I bring these words to inspire you, to hold the truth of who you are in your hearts so that you may inspire others to do the same. Read and re-read all the things I've told you and will tell you. There is an abundance that I want to tell you that is different than before, because the timing is different from before. I have always come to you in stages. Stages that would prepare you and cause you to ask questions of yourself. Each time has been a different group, nationality or social class. That is not so this time. I come for everyone to listen and heed my words. These words cross every boundary, every line and barrier. Let no man thirst for these words of God and not receive them. I will be silent no longer. You will begin to see my message strong and clear from every corner of the earth. It will be similar in context with slight variation, depending on the messenger. Bring forth your sick and heartbroken, and let them hear my words and be healed. Believe completely and all things will change.

LETTER 4

The sweet living waters of my Lord, grant me comfort in my times of need.
Your spirit ever so slightly touches me, so that I am permitted to feel.
Feel the completeness of who you are.
Pure and seeking endlessly to bring me closer to you.
My Lord, you never falter.
Your full beauty escapes me, yet I worry not, for I know each day you make yourself ever more evident in my life.

MY KINGDOM AWAITS EACH AND every one of you. I have accounted for all and there is a place for every man. It is not already written who shall come into oneness and who will not. Many are still deciding. When I gave you free will I gave you some difficult decisions to make. I gave you the choices that would shape your character and mend and save your souls. Many years have you been struggling with your choices and would have preferred I just make all of the decisions for you, but let me tell you why that could never be. You are too highly evolved for such a mandate. Misery would be rampant among you like the plagues of old. You feel you are in misery now, but listen when I say, be thankful for your choices, they hold the freedom that you seek. Commune with me that we might make the right choices together. Blessed will be your days when you follow the Lord.

Slow yourselves that you might concentrate on the processes your being must go through. You chose this course, now pay close attention. Your daily lives are so busy and full that you cannot attend to your soul. I ask that you would stop repeating again and again and again your same errors of ignorance in your life. Why do you insist on falling into the same traps and pitfalls? Those situations that drain you? You know immediately in your heart what those are because I have told you.

Wake up, my children, and clear your minds that you might hear. Your lives are not going to get better until you do. Just because it seems to be *right* for your neighbor to get into these situations does not make it *right* for you. You are my children. Start to act as if you know this before you waste too much time. Ascend your thoughts to me and me alone. *I* will bring you love like you have never known. *I* will bring you the prosperity you seek. The world will not give you those things. *I* will give you the peace that will not tolerate fear. Dear children, ask in prayer that my Holy Spirit, which I have given to you, wash over you like the waves, taking with it every doubtful thought, every negativity, any disease or illness; leaving behind my joy and my wholeness. Complete health and happiness is yours through the Spirit that brings it to you. This gift I have given to you. Do not take it without use of it. We take you in our arms at this time and just hold you, filling you with our strength and our complete love, for you feel weak and without power.

Know this to be true: you will have more power and more clarity than you ever thought possible. You only need your faith to see you through. I await our connection to begin again and to communicate once more.

Life is not meant to be difficult. Please do not be so insistent on making it so. Relax and heed not all that goes on around you. It will *all* wait and you will still be long ahead because of the moments you have chosen to spend with me. It is and always has been my good pleasure to supply all that you need and want. That has not changed. Reward yourselves with the *all of everything* that awaits you in heaven and on earth. Come to me.

Longsuffering can be ended with a word whispered on every man's lips . . ."Love." Let there be the words of love ringing through the air. Love can heal all wounds. It can create a new force and alliance among nations. Let it begin with you. Remember the words like a mantra throughout the day. *Let there be love, let there be love, let there be love.*

LETTER 5

*Y*OUR VALUE IS INCOMPREHENSIBLE TO you now. Do not try to understand the ins and outs of all we do, simply set aside yourself and go with what I am telling you each and every day. Long ago you each came to me with a mission of sorts. A burning in your soul to fulfill and be filled with Spirit here on earth. That desire has come to fruition and it pleases the heavens to see you lay down your will and open yourself to the light that will lead and show my children home. How fortunate you are to open the gift that has been given you. There lay the answer to all your questions. Share and not be silent for all of mankind is in need of these words. Your sole purpose at this time is to share the word and only the word of God, forsaking all else at this most important time. Your life as you know it will come back to you, but never as before. You will never be the same nor will you desire to be. Praise God for your gift and let it be known to all that God is a most loving and giving God. He does not cause distress or ill will. He loves you all so very much and delights in your joyfulness and right choices. Listen, Listen, Listen to the inner calling, wanting so desperately to be heard. Ever knocking on the doors of consciousness, ever so quietly giving you wisdom, asking for your participation along the way, asking for acknowledgement so that spirit can take you ever further along your path. Pay attention to that small, tender inner voice. You think it is your voice at times. Pray for discernment in this matter. Knowing one from another is the key. It is there, I promise you. I promised you Holy Spirit; I have not gone back on that vow. Do not push spirit away. Get quiet, have faith, and know that God seeks to commune with you through Spirit and will not rest until it is done. Have faith that is guiding you now.

LETTER 6

HY ARE MY CHILDREN so difficult to reach and commune with?

They have closed their eyes to the only way that is available to them. The only way to right choices and decisions. Your light can help them find a way. A process in which to follow and be diligent in. There is much to teach and be taught, so let's begin.

My Father has many mansions in which he has assembled a litany of angels to look after all of your earthly souls. Every angel having been charged with one or more souls to look after. Many times a deluge of angels will descend upon one soul, working in a large group to support one another, just as you do on earth at times. The reason for me telling you this is so you will all understand the workings of heaven, and get a bigger picture. Knowing all will help you make wiser decisions. There is a time in every person's life journey in which there is a crossroad. Don't be afraid to ask us for assistance. We are here around you, amongst you, waiting for your questions. For in the questioning is acknowledgement, acknowledgement that you really believe I am here. Love pours forth from us. Bring us your most important questions, your joys and celebrations as well. We share in your daily life; can we not share in it together? Always remember to praise my

Father. By doing so, you open up your own floodgates to happiness. Speak the words of gladness from your hearts. They were put there through the Spirit. Find them and use them. Glory to God!

I have not been selfish by keeping access to the Father all to myself. You are just as capable if not more so. Bring favor upon yourselves by listening to the words I say. Be forever mindful of the thoughts and words you say. Establish only those thoughts, which are loving, and kind to all people and nationalities. Heed the words "Love thy neighbor as thyself." Be long in understanding and short on doubt and un-forgiveness. Move forward in your relations with men of good faith and squander not what little time you have in my presence. Open up your doors and floodgates so that I may come in. Guiding you, strengthening you, holding you up, when you feel like falling. Look for ways in which your life is blessed. There is no need to notice your neighbor's blessings or feel as though they should be yours. Stay on your own path. You create excess problems in this way. Everlasting hope is yours to inherit from the heavenly beings that surround you. Stop turning the other way. The hope of the ages is yours. Embrace it.

We ask you to be with us, not against us. Flow with us each day. It is much easier than in the olden days. Your vibration as a people, a race, has risen to a place that we can contact and reach you much easier than before. As more and more of you become aware and believe, it will rise even higher. Believing and having faith that the old beliefs and attitudes can be admonished, and asking for the guidance and strength, your whole consciousness lifts. Beginning anew is all it takes. Seek my face throughout your days. Give yourself over to love of mankind and of all things. Lend yourself to a power much greater than yours. Of yourself you are nothing, but combined with the power of my Father within you are everything you desire to be. Lay down your will and hard hearts, lay them down on the altar of heaven. Fill thyself with the cup of heaven, the cup of understanding, and the cup of love. So be it.

LETTER 7

*F*ORGIVENESS IS NOT SUCH A tall order. It can be an automatic reaction to the pains and hurts you experience. The same with unconditional love; it can come as naturally to you as it does to all of us in heaven. Be present to your inner voice and all that it tells you. Immerse yourselves in the light and love that is rightfully yours. Claim it as a powerful gift that you can share and give to others.

LETTER 8

ᴇsᴛ ʏᴏᴜ ʙᴇ ʙᴏʀɴ ᴏғ the heavens, you shall not understand nor comprehend the vastness of our universe. Within this tiny nucleus in which you live is all that you could ever want and all that you can comprehend, but think bigger. Outside of your world is an even greater realm. There is life beyond your telescopes you will never see. Try to put yourselves in perspective to the greater picture as you go through your days. I will never say your days are not difficult, but they are certainly not worth creating so much havoc around. Your image of yourselves and your world is that of "greatest importance." That is as it should be, but remember . . . there are many such worlds equal in importance to yours. Treat yours with care and much love. It will not last forever. Times are changing rapidly. Consumption of your natural resources is at an all time high. Be gentle with her, your world; she cannot sustain for long. I urge scientists to combine their knowledge and resources, to join forces so that they may contribute to the greater good, glorifying God and themselves for they will never be forgotten because of their discoveries. Let the Spirit of God work through you and it will. Be diligent in writing your thoughts and ideas down as they immediately pop into your minds. Draw sketches and dimensions. Flow freely with the great anticipation of all that will spout forth from your scientific minds, knowing in your heart, believing that you are an instrument through which God works. Bow down, ridding yourselves of ego and self-importance, allowing God to express miracles through you. Modern day miracles they will be. Set forth with intention on this path you choose. Whosoever is not with me shall be working against me. Choose now and go forth in your chosen direction and do not look back.

To everyone I say, choose now the path your family will take, for you have the power to decide. Choose me, that you may reap rewards beyond your limited comprehension. You know not of the manna I can give you. Choose me now and experience and revel in the joy of it all. Lack will never be a part of your life. Do not even begin to doubt the power that reigns supreme in you once the decision has been made to follow me. Surrender your will to my will. Amen

LETTER 9

*H*OW LONG WILL YOU LET me weep? My heart breaks to see your world in turmoil. Your thoughtlessness for the affairs of your brethren troubles me. You speak highly of your connection with God yet you allow your brothers and sisters in Christ to go by the wayside. Have you no thought for anyone but yourselves? I have spoken through the ages, let no man harm another and then preach to the multitudes in my name. Blasphemers are you and shame will harbor in your hearts.

Make a list of all you know. A list of those you can help. The names that come to you in a fleeting moment telling you how you can help, write them down. Write down each name and beside it exactly what you will do for that person and when. This does many things. First, it is a great gift to the person you've touched. Second, you have opened up a channel within yourself to receive good from others as well as the blessings of heaven. Third, a shift will occur in you. You will begin to see and look for those opportunities in which you can help others. Your tenacity in this area will affect many others even if you do not notice. Praise God and give glory to him that gives you this life. Embrace it with passion. Life is truly a gift; begin to see it that way.

When the door of life swings wide, jump through. For I have prepared the path to hold and sustain you. Your test of faith will be in the jumping; having to know that it is I that calls you from the other side. Look for my light shining through to you, illuminating your whole being. Let my light heal you and take away any of the burdens you continue to hold on to. It is my will that I should shoulder them. Let them go. You will not step through the door unless you discard of them. Once this is done you will experience the feeling of weightlessness. You don't realize how heavy you truly are until this occurs. Revel in the feeling of light, stepping through to the God side of your life. All the instruction you need will be there for you. Do this now.

Everlasting love is yours. My promise of this I give to you, for in that promise lies forgiveness. **How can I love you unconditionally and not forgive every error or every sin you've committed.** Try this in your own dealings. It is simple if you commit to making it a way of life. I ask that you would not follow the way of the world on this matter. Be at the forefront. Be first to change. No matter what another does to you, love them unconditionally and forgive. In doing so you transform their lives as well as your own. Be this child of God that carries the word, glorifying God, and bringing peace upon yourselves.

Follow instinct, not the common man. Seek the fellowship of those on the same path as you for you may be tempted to discuss your affairs with those not of like mind, but I ask you to resist, for they may say things that will cause you to falter. Always keep your eyes and thoughts on me. Share with those men that have no God the glory and joy God has brought into your life, but do not seek advice from these men. If they give it freely without being asked, hold it from you and graciously thank them, quickly moving back into your God center. Their intentions are not always bad, but you must remain focused if you are to carry out this work. Do not expel anyone from your life, but put on the armor of God when you are around those of negativity. Your souls are tender and need protection from the possible negative influences of others. Like I have said before, they are not always intentional, but harmful just the same. Safeguard yourselves so that there will be no question as for whom you stand.

My Father in heaven, hallowed by thy name, thy kingdom come thy will be done on earth as it is in heaven.

LETTER 10

EAUTY I SEE IN ALL the world and in all things. Can you see it? I call forth all my good children to see and understand from whence this beauty has come. We are a family built on the foundations of love for one another. Within the loving is the beauty of it all. My people, you are so blessed. Blessed in knowledge, blessed in abundance that is all about you. Give praise to the one that has blessed you so. Praise him every hour of every day that you might know the giver of all things more intimately. It is not the Father's wish to receive such praise, but in doing so you, the children, would have a greater peace.

Be still and quiet your minds. A long time ago I came to you with the voice of angels trumpeting the news of a forgiving God. I ask you now to remember and study upon those words. Take them into your hearts and into your days, filling your hearts with joy. Your mission is to free yourselves from all that binds you. Hatred binds you, lack of forgiveness binds you, and doubt and poverty bind you. All that I have come to tell you speaks in ways to lessen the burdens and lift your soul and spirit. Lessen the shame you feel over the sins "you think" you have committed. Our Father does not judge in the ways you think. Your human minds have no comprehension of what our Father is like.

Now is the time for a shift, the time for a huge shift in consciousness to occur . . . now, today, not tomorrow.

This is a call to order. Let us get our affairs in order now so that we can spring forth a new life and a new world. A place of unconditional love where race and gender have no precedence. A place where your children are safe. Your belief is that it can never be, but it can, through you. You are the beginning of it all. One heart at a time can be transformed through your actions. Let go of your human self and embrace your God light, that God self within. Be obedient and your whole self changes.

Your time together on earth is all about making this happen. Universal changes will begin to take place, then global, all from the shifts you are making in your personal lives. Heaven on earth awaits you. How soon do you want your children to experience it? I am here, ready to express greater things still. It is such an exciting time. The energy is high and ready to explode in anticipation of it all. Can you feel the tingling in your body when we speak the truth? Phenomenal lives are ahead of you. Heed my words so that you may be free of all that binds and move through to living a true life with God by your side.

LETTER 11

Extreme confidence I have in all of you to carry out my work, bringing a higher awareness to the world. This higher awareness I speak of will be a time of great turmoil for many. It will mean changing every element, every way of thinking and doing. Not every man would wish this to be so, but for those who are ready and prepared, it will be an easy exchange and a readily accepted one. In this time of change many miracles will occur within time and space as well as within yourselves. Be ready to accept them. Prepare your bodies and minds for the Second Coming of our Lord. It will not be as you've been led to believe or imagined. The fiery teachings of the past should be left in the past. Your new world is ready for a new understanding. You are evolving at a quickened pace and the Second Coming is through your consciousness, not the flesh. God will call upon his people and you will be made ready through Holy Spirit and will ascend into higher awareness and the heavens here on earth will be made manifest. Holy Spirit will reign eternal and will sweep through the land with a mighty wind. Fear not, good people, my Spirit comes not to persecute, but to wield its power and elevate the minds of all men, young and old. The body of Christ will live in all that would accept it.

Be ye kind one to another. Realizing that all are one, through God living within you. Long have I awaited this time and again I say the time is now. Fill your hearts and minds with thanksgiving for those things, which are about to come. I will share with you later what those are, for now be content to know that I and my Father will rain down upon the earth in love and complete understanding to guide you to a new level of being. These words are truth I speak. Forgotten are the words I spoke of long ago to a people not quite ready to hear. I will not be shut out or turned off, I will be heard now more than ever before. Locusts and plagues are not needed now, but hear me well, I will be heard and not lost to a lower vibration, a lesser self or lower consciousness. Follow the Christ nature, the God self and tarry not in anxiousness or concern of what is to come. It is all written. Gladness and Glory will abound.

LETTER 12

STOP HAVING THOSE CONVERSATIONS AMONGST yourselves concerning livelihood. Has not your Father always been serving you all of your lives, placing abundance at your feet? Go now with a joyous heart and find that which would serve you best. You do yourselves and others a great disharmony when complaining about your livelihood. It is OKAY to begin again, even if it is the hundredth time. Be glad in the job at hand or complete it and begin anew. A gift that has been given is the ability to start over at any time. The stories are too numerous to tell of all who felt a calling late in their lives so strong that they launched new lives in an utterly euphoric manner.

Children, remember the Son, and remember the life he led so that you would know the greatness within you. Do not push it aside because you do not feel greatness. It is there only to be rediscovered.

Verily I say unto you, go forth this day in constant prayer.

LETTER 13

WITH THE EVER-PRESENT HOLY SPIRIT about you, you can easily go about the tasks at hand. No matter how mundane or trivial they become, Spirit lifts you above the monotony of it, changing your attitude to one of longsuffering, patience and love. Give up your lasting obsession of constant stimulus. There is no doubt that is why many can never hear the guidance my Father has to give to you. Take time to listen with complete silence. Put away all distractions. Hear me crying out to you in torrents. What you do not know is that you have heard me before, but had no idea it was I. Pray for discernment. Discernment of the voices in your mind and discernment of dreams. Pray for magnification of these voices and a strong intuition so that there will be no doubt, whatsoever, that it is I that speaks to you. I will be speaking a truth to you that has been lost along the way.

Go inside yourself and quietly choose a dream you had when you were young. It can be anything large or small. Something you wanted to be, something you wanted to own, but did not achieve or get. Imagine yourself as a young child dreaming that dream. Visualize all the details around it. Hold it close and feel the emotion behind attaining it. Breathe . . . and take one step today in attaining that for yourself, just one step. Tomorrow take another. It is not an accident that this dream should be given to you at a young age. Your whole life has been about attaining it.

I speak very clearly to children. They know what they want and they have no concept of time or responsibility. They know it should come to them and no adult should tell them otherwise. Do not break the spirit of your young ones. That does not mean spoil them; only let them dream and work towards those dreams. I've spoken clearly to you as well, before you began filtering me out of your lives. You were all young once. Try to remember the dreams I placed upon your hearts. I am with you now and it is OKAY to dream your dreams, but it is better to live them.

LETTER 14

LET NOT YOUR HEARTS BE saddened; my call to glory is forthcoming. You may not know the way as yet, but it is just beyond the wall of understanding. All will be shown to you at the precise time. You are saviors in your own right and will bring many of my children to the light. Forsake me not, but allow me to work miracles through you. If I told you to preach, what would you preach? If I told you to heal, how would you heal? Only through faith that God can do all these things through you, and not as you, will it be done. There is nothing to do, only believe. Begin to touch others in need and say a quick prayer stating their truth. You know it is within you; let it out. Your beliefs are strong within you, let them out. There are those who need to hear. You are healers of mind and body. Let it out and know your truth in the process.

LETTER 15

*Y*OUR LEVEL OF UNDERSTANDING MULTIPLIES in the face of adversity. By going through each trial you become more understanding of yourselves, others and the ways of the Father. Do not blame God for your unfortunate circumstances. Look at yourself first before anyone else. You will be the one responsible. In these trials, you have the opportunity to make decisions either from a positive nature or a negative one. The positive side will hold you in the light, not the darkness. Let your thoughts ascend to a higher place daily asking for guidance on those decisions. Be forewarned, evil (error) thoughts lurk in the minds of men and that is why your thoughts must go to a higher realm for guidance.

You must be one in the knowledge that I am all things and knowing that through faith you can become perfect according to the measure of Christ within us, allowing that Christ to be our guide. Do not allow others to lead you astray from the divine guidance within you. Do not go with the whims and teaching of others, but be steadfast and sincere in your love and understanding of your own knowing. Each man is so different. See it for them, but do not render opinions. Hold steadfast to the idea that we can all become Christ-like, closer to perfection in daily life. Co-creating a beautiful life, all through blind and complete faith that it can and will be done through Holy Breath and God the Father. Belief is the core of all things expressed in your lives. Many of the things I've said to you about love, forgiveness, and harmony are foundations to begin changing your beliefs so that we can begin changing your lives, hence changing your world.

LETTER 16

RAY TO THE LORD YOUR God expecting miracles to be preformed in your life. Glory on high, he receives joy in seeing your blessings manifest. Lift up thine eyes to the heavens keeping ever focused on God. Do not stray to the left or right, but listen to your guidance, the inner knowing. The love of God fills you through the Spirit as well. Let your whole life be a living prayer to God. Speak to him constantly throughout the day. God the Father will lead you to the most beautiful places. I see him leading you to one now. Let go of all that holds you back and take his hand. Your judgments, jealousies, spite and the need to be right are all holding you down. You cannot fly with the angels until the hold is loosened. Evaluate your every move, your every thought. Begin a new way of thinking.

Shatter the old paradigm you've been urged to live all your lives. Open the new door to freedom and expression. By doing so you are opening up to my divine spirit. It is time to change. As prophesied many years ago the time is now. I come to you with more love and more understanding than ever before. Make way, for my ways will lead you home to that place of perfect peace. I am your friend and brother in Christ. I can show you the way.

Put down your false faces and show all who you really are. The great things you are made of need to be shown. It does man no good to see its worldly reflection in you. It needs to see God in you so that it might reflect back the God inside of them. Halleluiah! You will change before mine eyes. The heavens rejoice again and again as the flock is called home to serve. Blessed be the children that have faith enough to lose all their masks and live in God and he in them, blindly accepting that their faith in the Father is all they need. Let me deliver you from the worries you face. I am no less my Father's Son in doing so and so it is with you. You were not meant to carry such burdens and strife. Bundle them all and hand them to me. I refuse to give them back. Clear your minds now and worry not. If in this you believe, I will take care of it all for you.

LETTER 17

*L*AY BLAME ON NO ONE for the unfortunate circumstances you find around you. Through many years has this earth been transforming and many more will come. You have been taught to fear and negate your own feelings. As a whole your customs are laughable in the sight of God. Each group having their traditions and rituals, forgetting that there is service work to be done. There are men, women, and children mentally and emotionally starving. Many of them are in your own communities. Bring these children to the Light for their healing. Help them through their difficulties through your presence and love. Forget your traditional ways and love one another. Be gentle with one another and always put God first. Our love is so great that in order for you to receive your fill you must give it away, making room for the overwhelming light that we offer. Changing the smallest of intentions within yourselves each day can change your circumstances. Laugh with us, cry with us, share every moment with us. We are here to share in it all with you. You may not see, but you will feel my arms around you when you need comfort, or my smile when you are joyous. These things and more you will feel as we commune together. Your vibrations will rise to that of the heavens the more you consciously spend time with me. It is my greatest wish to be and live through you. To make you whole and bless the lives of others through all the great works we can perform. For so long I have wanted and waited for this relationship with my beloved ones. I am more complete in the process as well.

Forgive the day I call you to service for it will never be complete. It brings forth more beauty and understanding, but takes tenaciousness. Have you got what it will take to change the world, my children? Do you have the strength? Draw it from me now and henceforth. Your message and light goes forth to nation upon nation. Kings and servants alike will heed my words and their call to God's glory, forsaking all else to live by the hands of God. Force will not be an issue but that of free will to do with these words as you would choose to do. Be ready for what awaits you and your children; the bridge that closes the gap between here and eternity. The bridge cannot be broken for truth is the strength that holds fast. Give up your falseness and cling to what holds true. Remember, your truth will set you free.

My Father sends vestiges of angels to hold you up with courage and strength. Acknowledge their presence that you may feel a greater strength within you.

Prepare in these things I have told you so that you will move easily to a more beautiful life. This is not meant as drudgery, but as life sustaining. Put on your royal garments of Godliness and harbor no shame in doing so. Let your love shine brightly as we in heaven support and lift you up. The phoenix and the dove live in harmony in the glorious days to come. How is it man cannot see to do the same? Harmony with one another is of utmost importance. This includes your animals and plant life. Breathe in the air of life and see peace with every living thing. You depend on one another for life, be gentler than before and strive endlessly for harmony.

Be of good cheer now and in the days to come. Heavy is my heart when I see the destruction that has occurred to your world as well as your physical bodies. You have no idea the blessing it was to be able to have an earthly form. You give no regard to your bodies and treat them as though they would never fail. God's graciousness is with you in this respect, giving you much more strength and longer lives than would seem possible according to the way you treat yourselves. I do not come to preach about your health only to remind you to take good care. Be mindful of your blessings. Let nothing stand in your way of complete happiness. Health is but one step to getting there. I look forward to the day when you can feel the freedom of being without physical form and delight in the radiant light that you are becoming. Through study and prayer the light becomes stronger. Through service of all good things it becomes stronger. Through love and forgiveness of others it becomes stronger. Living in harmony with all things creates an even larger, more brilliant light. Embrace all of these things into your life and your radiance will illumine the heavens and all of those around you.

Oh beautiful spirit, fear not, the darkness always bends to the day. It is I that will accompany you on your journey ahead. Take my hand, wherever you go and you will not be alone. Priceless is our time together. I attempt to be your every breath, your every thought, your life. Let it be done according to your faith and belief in me.

My love for you runs deep. You grace me with your presence. Your warmth surrounds me placing a tender smile upon my lips. Your insatiable beauty has lifted me beyond the comprehensions of my own mind into another place and time. My lofty goals and ambitions are minute in comparison to the world you've shown me. I am overwhelmed with gratitude for all you've given and expressed. My faith burns strong and the ability to know you at such an intense level is incredible to me. At last my truth is evident. I pray the light in my life never leaves me.

By being a beacon of light, others begin to recognize emotions and feelings within themselves that have been hidden for years. As spoken of earlier, the importance of remembering your childhood dreams plays an important role here. Remembering the dreams of a child, faith of a child and love of a child will bring about the understanding of truth. Go back to the time when you forgot. It is so simple yet you make it so hard. Place your ego-self on the altar and go back to remembering who you are. Within each of you is the soul's code, the seed that holds your truth. Nourish it and it will bloom, even until long after you are gone from this earth. Man as we know it will not reign supreme over this earth forever. Many unnatural and supernatural beings will call this earth home. There will be with them an uncanny ability to understand each one's soul and see long into the future. They will have a deep harmony about them and the way they live. Showing you this shares a vision of what man will evolve to. These are not aliens I speak of but descendants evolved from you, the people of earth, the children of God. Let us hold the vision of a greater peace and a greater understanding of one another.

LETTER 18

How shall I take the human race to the glories of heaven? Should I stay silent and allow this existence to continue? Not all are in such a state and those are the ones I call to action to help their brethren who are in need of it. Why do I speak now instead of letting all of mankind go about their pre-destined course? Because not all is pre-destined. There are many things undecided and are left to you, the all of mankind, to figure out. I come to give you guidance and hope along with simplistic steps to help along the way. Be aware that it is not always easy, but continue to keep your eyes on the Lord. Your greatest mountains cannot keep you from what you desire lest you lose faith. I will let you know the time and place to take action, but for now just be in my presence and allow me to do the workings in your heart. Stay still my young servants. I will show you the way. At long last I have found the importance of being loved by my people. I delight in my Father's love, but now a new love is erupting from my people, to me, in mass. The difference will be a greater number will know and understand the changes coming, giving comfort to those who do not understand. I am omnipotent, but the love I receive from you creates a way of non-resistance. A path more clearly defined and the people will be made ready to hear. All of you are important, do not lose sight of that.

There was a man of great wealth and he was asked to lay down his ego and his pride by God. The man could not see his way clear to do so and died. Did he perish by the hand of God?

His pride was so great that having consumed his mind, body, and soul there was nothing of value left to allow him life. Take care and keep your soul in balance. Others will recognize your imbalance long before you will. Listen for the discordance in your heart and relations with others. See where excessive pride might play a part in your own life. Lay it down and resist the temptation to pick it up again. There is no room for ego and the full light of God. Make your choices carefully that you may live fully with great joy and happiness. You may look good to the world, but the heavens and I know what's going on inside; hurt, anger, remorse, and an emptiness that should be filled with God and no other thing or possession. Each and every day trying to fill the void. Stop! Just stop and let me fill the void; by asking, you will receive your guidance and help. You are extremely powerful in your own rights and do not need the things in which you indulge. Live lighter than ever before, by losing the heaviness in which you insist on carrying you will be freed. This enables you to live a much lighter existence and you can experience it; allowing you to laugh and enjoy life more than you ever thought possible. My children, you are the light of the world. Let it shine.

LETTER 19

*W*HAT SHALL I WRITE ABOUT a Son's love for his people? The depth and breadth of it is so far reaching that you cannot comprehend. If I love you so, why do I let you suffer? So caught up in your pain it is difficult to see the reasoning. I do not allow nor wish you harm. Within you is the power to choose light instead of darkness. Each of you has that power. Ask me for the strength and it shall be done. In your darkest days you cannot understand, but once you have emerged victorious from the darkness you will know and be clear as to why each situation and circumstance has occurred. If your ultimate goal is to become one in Christ spirit, then we must all be of one mind and understand the trials of one another. The choices you have in reacting to negative situations are great. You can choose to approach these things from a very dramatic and victimized place or you can choose a position of strength and gratefulness. Life is much easier from a position of strength. Do not give the world permission to victimize you. Stand strong in your belief in God and in yourselves. Be forever grateful. Even if you can only find one thing to be grateful for, hold it up in gratitude and from that one thing, others will come. A very special gift arises from such an attitude. It is called happiness. The secret has been unleashed. Now run and use it at will. None of my messages have ever been difficult, quite the opposite. Why then is it such a burden to live a Christ-filled life?

These are my words to live by:

Pray every day, all day
Share the joys and sorrows
Love thy neighbor, have forgiveness always in
your heart.
Do not judge and live in harmony with all.
Make right choices and be forever grateful.
These are the words of the Lord.

LETTER 20

BE PATIENT; YOU KNOW NOT what the Father has in store for you. Be true to yourselves in all of your dealings and God will take care of the rest. Have faith. Comfort those who come to you in sadness and emotional turmoil. Even when they are unhappy with you do not let them take your energy down to where they are and want you to be. Arm yourself with the power of God and speak your truth. If you have been a friend in good faith state it so and move on. What they are experiencing is merely for you to touch, not become a part of. Agree to handle any loose ends on your part, and then cordially depart. Again, your vocation is not meant to be drudgery but an avenue of prosperity and flexibility so that you can go about God's work. Your voice is needed to shout from mountaintops, but not yet. There is still much to learn and the pieces have not been put in place. Go about your daily affairs and it will be shown to you, all this is waiting for you. Let go of fear in your life, then you will have the strength of the angels.

LETTER 21

*A*T THE END OF DAYS your lord shall be triumphant. The power entrusted to you and the armies of heaven will reign victorious. Spirits of all kinds will cower back to the depths of darkness from whence they came. Keep this vision alive by being a messenger of good and light to all that you know and meet. I, as always, will give you the words in which to commence.

Our heavens prepare and ready themselves for battle, calling forth all souls that would join in truth and love to raise up the error-filled ways of earth. I will begin in the churches of old. Sanctity and loyalty has been destroyed and so will the church be. Pray now for the forgiveness of your souls, O pious ones. Your suffering will be long lived. To others of the cloth, I say do not condemn my children to a hell of your own making. I came to show the world an everlasting love and peace. It is not my Father's wish to see such guilt and sadness instilled upon his children. Be forewarned, change the message that burns and quench their thirst with the new word; my word which is truth. However slight at first, but change at once. Your hearts are in the right place; just change the direction your messages are going. Leave behind the ways of old and come running with anticipation and joy into what is to be. What you have not seen, but have heard prophecy, is the best yet to come. Follow, my children, and you will see the plagues of old disappear, allowing for a new way, a new day upon this earth; a day of understanding, a day of reckoning and a day of agape love.

Fierce storms will set in motion a time like no other. Volcanoes will flow, the seas will rage and the winds of change will be upon you. Mystified are my people and rightfully so. It is not like my Father to send such force; it is your path spoken of long ago. Do not be saddened by the loss to come. It is as it should be. Comfort your hearts and those of others. Your strength is paramount in these times. Take the time to regain that strength through communication with the Christ. At long last a peace will come. The heavens will open up around you. A great light will appear in the sky and you will know it is me, the living Son of God, come once again to call my people home. Home into the fold of the Christ Spirit. Ascension will be possible, but not by all. Many will want to stay on earth to help and comfort loved ones. Others will not have a choice but to stay behind. Many will come to me and the Father, who await them in heaven. The numbers will be great on both accounts. Multitudes of heavenly bodies will descend upon the earth to assist those left behind through guidance and prayer, lifting them up so that they might find their way through the myriad of questions and socio-economic turmoil. Lose not your focus on the Lord. Whence I have come to say pray upon these things and straighten your way lest you be left behind also. There is nothing to fear if you believe. If you are faltering, go and see your way clear to believe in me, the Lord thy God, and all that it entails. I am the Son fo God, the still inner knowing, I am the light of the Almighty God! He who believes in me will not perish but have this everlasting life.

LETTER 22

ROM THE BEGINNING OF TIME I've come to you with open arms, asking to be by your side. Many of you welcome me and my Son into your daily lives and I am so grateful for that. It is truly our greatest pleasure to be part of your lives. It is the ones that do not seek our companionship and oneness that I am trying to reach now in this passage.

Lay down your human selves letting go of your anger at life, your un-forgiveness of what others have done to you. It is okay without this outer wall you have created for defense. That is exactly what holds you prisoner. I know there are days and even weeks that go by when you are fine, but I also hear the days when you cry out to the heavens and beat your chest with frustration and anger, and sadness. Weary are your souls from trying to control and manipulate life. There is no longer need for you to do this. Give it all to me, your worries and the anxieties of life. Any problem great or small, lay it upon my altar, which I shall not ignore. These are the words of the Lord. I will send a sign, a message, a charter to guide you. Look for it. Seek those around you who are blessed with my anointing so that you may ask them for guidance in your time of need. Surround yourselves with people of Christ mind so that you will not falter, slipping back into your earthly ways. You are a child of God. Recognize this and claim it into your lives as truth. I do not allow nor do I want suffering for my people. It is only in your wrong thinking that you suffer.

There are those that would ask, "How can wrong thinking include such things as rape, killing, etc.?" Let me answer by saying there are forces that inhabit the minds and bodies of man and cause horrible situations to occur, things no person should have to endure, but listen when I say I come to take the victims long before they suffer. You leave your body when defiled in such ways and know the comfort of heaven before it is done. I do not ask for understanding, it is too much for you to understand, the pain too great. Once again, do not shoulder the burdens alone. Let me take them from you. There will always be those insensitive to your pain. They know not what you go through and cannot even imagine how to react. Have pity on them as well. Gain strength from those who love you and want to help you. Allow them to do it. It helps them as well as you.

Life can be altered by many of the difficulties you encounter. Do not allow those difficulties to extinguish life. Bring peace to yourself by letting the Christ show you truth and guide you in every situation. Ask what the underlying reasons are behind each situation. Have you been a part? Has your positive or negative outlook had anything to do with it? Ask God what part you can play in making it better for all parties. The hardest part of asking is following through on what you're told. Many times what you hear will make no sense at all or even seem relevant. Trust and follow through anyway. It is in the obeying that the true blessing comes. Make sense of it later.

LETTER 23

*W*ITHIN ME ARE MANY PATHS to God, and the same is with you. Choose carefully the path you take; choose the path of right thinking. You should feel whole and have a clear mind, having no doubts that the way you choose is correct. Don't forget to pray and listen for the answers. I do not mean that the right way is always the easiest. That is not always so. Many times obstacles frequent the path, but are easily overcome by the power of my Father and I. We work through you to achieve and express great things. The Father and I are one and long to be in oneness with you. When this happens, great things happen. Look at the great writers of your time; it is not of their own accord that they deliver such messages and philosophies. It is the oneness we share with them. It is the same with many of your artists, musicians, and business leaders of the day. They are clear about their purpose, their way and their oneness with God. They know they are nothing without the Father who lives in them. All of the great spiritual leaders who speak truth have known this as well. It is your time to know your path to greatness is through the Father. It is time for your oneness to occur. Do not hold your tongue, but speak truth. Pray the prayer of everlasting knowledge that the words you speak are not of your own but those of your Father in heaven. Glory abounds this day! Feel the words come to your lips like rain drops falling, each word in perfect place, quenching the thirst of all who hear. How can I keep from you the truths of heaven?

This is my way of communication. There are many forms in which I appear, but the spoken word is most effective in reaching the hearts of man. Never coerce the message for it will always come from a higher source. Prepare first in prayer and thanksgiving and then ready your thoughts on God and it will be given to you. From whence do man's thoughts originate? Pure and unattached, they are from God. Anything less is from man's lower vibration. Keep focusing on the higher vibrations of God's love, God's peace and understanding, God's grace and forgiveness. Keep a higher vision for yourself; one of Godliness. It can be attained in your lifetimes. There is only one Jesus the Christ, but there will be many Christed children.

Heed my call and come home into the folds of Christ service. Thinking only how you can be of service to others and not of yourself. Change the focus from you to mankind. Always focus on God's children in need. This is from where your spiritual manna comes.

LETTER 24

LOSE SELF AND ALL THINGS will be given unto thee.

How can the promise be delivered if you do not?

You of your human self cannot receive the gifts I offer. Only in setting aside your human wants and desires and reaching for God can you receive them; and when you do discover the miracles in your life, be grateful. With a glad heart rejoice in your blessings. It can and will change you on every level. By God changing one life at a time, the universe quickens to a time of understanding. A glorious time! Your actions now will ready all of you for the beauty to come. I am here now to prepare you for it. Some will call this ludicrous, others insane. My people will recognize it as truth.

O that the hardhearted among you would open your minds to the Lord and drink in the possibilities of a better time and place, where God the good reigns eternal. To bask in his light and love, fearing nothing. The beauty of it all is beyond measure. The heavens wait in joyous anticipation for the days of love and peace, where heaven and earth collide. Humans and spirit alike will dwell upon the earth in full knowledge of one another. Holy Spirit is always here now, but will be more visible at this time because you will be more receptive to its presence. All of man will know this force of power among you. Clear your hearts and minds and make way for the dove of peace to enter and transform you.

Can you find the Garden of Eden within you? Search diligently, for it is in everyone. You posses layer upon layer of consciousness and thought. The garden lies beneath them all. Deeper and deeper you must go before reaching it. Once there, you will never be the same. Ask for guidance, enjoy the journey and when the garden is found, enjoy life to its fullest without reserve. In the garden your complete truth can be found. A reflection where you can really see yourself and who it is you truly are, your complete one-ness with God. No lack, no fear, where all is provided. You now understand the all of everything, because you are one with it. All of it is available to you, only begin the search. Where there is one that finds this garden within, there will be another, then another, then another. A great mass will find and recognize their divinity, this divine right that belongs to all men. This will lift the energies of the earth to greater good. Believe in earth as a place of peace and it will be done. Believe you can be a part of it and it will be done. Each one of you makes a difference to the universal consciousness. That is how important you are to the Father and the effect you have on the world.

How important are the ideas and notions of mankind compared to the harmony of ideas presented by God? How incredible it is to see you, day after day after day, struggling over and over again with their same ideas and strategies. Why do you insist on making the same mistakes over again? We come in clarity to you now to show you the way that there might be no more struggling in your lives. Peace is your right. Claim it now and move forward through your life. Let us hold your hand and let us walk through the Garden of Eden together. Our love for you runs deep. Allow yourself to live fully and completely, discovering along the way the essence of you. What is it you are made of and what were your intentions for yourself on earth? You can reclaim who you truly are and let it shine into the world like a beacon from Heaven. For that is truly the essence of who you are; a heavenly beacon of light to shine hope and glory into the world. Breathe in the Christ light that belongs to you. Only beauty lies before you on your path to God. Breathtaking are the views that come before you.

Gentle spirit, praise God for these blessings promised but not yet seen. In your gratitude you will glimpse the glorious road ahead. I am the seeker of heaven on earth. I am the beloved. Take me into your arms embrace.

LETTER 25

*Y*OU ARE FORGETTING WHO I am. I am the provider of all things; I am the giver of gifts and light. I am your every prayer whispered in the silence of your minds. Remember the solace I give when you are in need of it. Forget not the days and nights I watch over you, giving you love and peace. Face each new day with the understanding that I go before you to greet the day. I do not leave you, but stay by your side always. Gentle is your spirit when I am near. Peace is yours; only ask. That peace which begins with you will grow and spread. Be the vine that grows from one place to another spreading peace yet gently disrupting the garden's usual way of growing. Allow your light to ever so slightly shine in the presence of darkness. With my touch upon your words you can cause a change of great magnitude to occur. Do not proclaim like thunder, but as the softness of rain. I prepare thee for God's work and not man's. Continue your daily time with me so that I may show you guidance along the way.

Exaltation! Bring forth your love and understanding of all people and nations. It is much needed, for you will not feel like loving and understanding, but you have to. It is *your* right decision, the right thinking for who *you* are. It is not an easy task, but life altering once done. Take these words into your heart. Think on them and discover how you can begin to use truth to make a difference in your life and the many lives of others around you. There are multitudes of people who need to know the word of God. Give them hope that they might see clearly with their own eyes, and feel, with passion, all that I have to give them. For all their searching the way is still clouded. Paint the picture so they might recognize their God selves and their higher vision when it is placed upon them. Speak forcefully and with conviction the words I have given you. Pray over the masses for healing and clarity of the message you bring.

The presence of the Lord is great and will inhabit the earth. Doors will not be closed to the words I have come to say. The great white spirit sweeps from heart to heart, house to house, readying the minds of men for the word made manifest. As you are this day, in your present day circumstance, none of you would be ready for these great things I speak of. In time, my Holy Spirit will descend upon the earth quickening your thoughts and ideas. Then will you be ready to receive the greatest gifts of God. The word of the Lord will make sense, flowing like fountains from young and old. The visions of peace and understanding that I speak of will become clear as you see and understand exactly how it can be done. Step forth in celebration now for what is to come and take my words to heart. Study upon them and integrate them into your lives so that all who are willing will be ready. Feel the love of a thousand heavenly beings pouring over you. How can you deny yourself that love? Verily I say once more, lay down your earthen souls and pick up your true self so that I may speak to you, be with you, work through you, all the rest of your days. Placing your way into my way, I take over for you now. Let go . . . let go . . .

Be thee still as a summer rain allowing my presence to pour over you. My light penetrates every part of your soul. Relax and feel the weightlessness that comes from my presence, lifting and supporting you. Let your mind be still with a knowing that I am near. What does it feel like to know I am with you? What is it like? What words am I speaking to you now?

"My sweetest brothers and sisters in Christ, you have not disappointed me. Do not look away in shame, but gaze upon my face and know you are mere children in the sight of God."

LETTER 26

To KNOW GOD IS TO know love. All that is love is God. Who of you does not want to know love? It causes weightlessness, a euphoria and light-headedness. Love is strength that can conquer any demons you hold. By putting love first you put God first. I will carry judgment of character, not you one for another. Only show acceptance and love for one another. Find your way to help those in need. Are they not your brothers and sisters in Christ? Do not turn away because you think yourself better than them. You are the same. One day you will know this to be true. Touch the lives of others; don't continue to look straight ahead with blinders on. Look them in the eyes and show them the love within you. There is no rhyme or reason but the love you share today passes on exponentially. It changes lives. It makes the difference. Never think you are worth nothing. You are everything perfect and whole in God's eyes. Mistakes will always be made. Do not allow yourself to look back; only move forward. Keep looking ahead at your higher vision for yourself. Make peace, but never a backward glance. Your body and mind will become clearer as you throw away the old and make room for the new. You have held on long enough to the clutter in your minds. It is time to rejuvenate, clearing out negative perceptions, judgment, pessimism, doubt and unclean thoughts. Just as you touch many with your love you touch just as many with your negativity. Sweep the piles from your mind and polish it with new thoughts that give light to you and those around you.

Acceptance and love should be your new way of thought. Assuredness and optimism should pave your way. A new life you will have created for yourselves and all within the power and confines of your own mind. Halleluiah!

I have sent my Son to proclaim to you a message of love and truth. You have mocked me with your manmade rules and tributaries. I do not need your pomp and circumstance and your cathedrals of stone and gold. The glory of God comes from the love of the children not the egotism of the church elders. Pray that those of you I address would lose their sense of self-importance. Their sense of helping the lowly, ignorant ones get closer to God through them. Pray that this ends. My good people do not allow it. Take control of your own spirituality, letting no man tell you what rites to perform. I am the way shower, the truth and the light. I am your example. No man shall enter the kingdom of heaven, but by my example. The belief in that will show you the way Ask and I will show you .

My life as a child was scrutinized by all, wanting to see in the flesh the prophecy made real. At this young age I was completely aware of my connection with Source. Later I was to know this was God. I studied under my father Joseph and my mother Mary for many years, daily communing with my Father in heaven asking, "Is it time, is it time for me to teach the multitudes of your heavenly grace?" The answer was always no until I had communed and learned enough to begin my message of love and hope.

I tell you these things so you would know that I was

never a true Son of Man, but always Son of God. I knew my Christed nature all throughout my life. Do not discard me as fantasy, but believe in me.

Letter 27

*I*T IS IN MY PRESENCE that you will find hope, freedom and justice. What do I mean by the three of
these? I say they are important elements in a true life. To
find and know hope where there is none. To obtain freedom from fear, doubt, and loneliness. To create a life that
is just and fair to all. These are some of the things I wish
for you.

There are so many ways to incorporate all that I teach
into your lives. Never just one way that never changes.
Your lives and their evolution are all about change. Those
who will not change are left behind. You must make way
for the new ways of worship and the new ways of thinking, to help you move closer to God. I have sent messenger after messenger to alleviate your confusion and you are
still engrained in your traditions and chatter.

Seek all of me in my entirety, not just within your
churches and holy sanctuaries. I am beside you at every
moment. I am within you upon every call. It is not I who
has forsaken you. It is you who has forgotten what life
with me is like. You have pushed me aside in pursuit of
your greater things, yet I am a forgiving God and love you
just the same for doing so. Fill your heart with gladness
for you will know without a doubt that I am your Father
giving you the blessings of heaven. You know what those
blessings are yet you feel you would be better served by
worldly blessings. Seek ye first the kingdom of heaven.

Place your eyes upon your Lord and all else will be given unto you. It is a leap of faith, but it is also required. You are either for me, or against me. Strengthen your faith in the Lord who blesses you. Do not take a step without first consulting me, the God within your heart and mind. Allow me to be of service in helping you attain all that your hearts desire. Put me to the test; I will not fail you. Blessed are those who can set aside their lives to follow the Christ life, in faith, believing all things are from God and will be taken care of. Have I not mentioned these things to you before? Many of you are on the fence regarding this matter. You are the ones who know in your heart I am calling you, but cannot see clear to answer. The worldly hold is too strong.

LETTER 28

Y HEART BURNS WITH THE desires in your heart. My heart aches with the sadness in your heart. Take up your burdens and walk with me to a place of compassion and grace. Believing in me will make the difference in your lives. Allow me to work there for you. You still think I am not there for you, and think I do not talk with you, but I do. You feel the thoughts I give you are irrelevant or ignorant in nature because you do not know they come from me. They do not come with a sign to acknowledge them. The more in tune with self you are the easier to hear those thoughts. They are subtle, almost fleeting, in your mind. Be aware of them as you go into prayer and meditation. As you ask questions notice it is I that answers. Ask and you will receive guidance from Holy Spirit. Be forewarned; I come not in judgment but in quiet resolve. Be gentle with yourselves when mistakes are made. Move on and start anew. Peace comes, sometimes slowly, but yet it will come. See there in the distance a great many blessings coming upon you. Fear not what the future will be, but revel in the possibilities in which you will create. Flow in joy and happiness from one experience to the next. It is not always as bad as you imagine. Remember, I am on the other side leading you home. Be still and know that I am God speaking to you through spirit in ways you can understand and comprehend. There is so much greatness that you will one day know of. You are part of the greatness, but do not know of it as yet.

Beseech the living God in you to come forth and bless all those who might receive it. Mighty are my words for they will touch many. The heavens are alive with anticipation of the changes being brought forth. Halleluiah! Let not your hearts be saddened. I am near to you always. Step forth in faith to tell the world theses things that I have told you. Each one is responsible for making the change within them, but only after first hearing the word spoken. Do not hold a man responsible if he has never heard of me. Share with him all that you know and hold nothing back. I take over in his life after that. Much responsibility lay with my people to share the words I speak so that all men have the same knowledge and opportunity to experience the love and peace that we know and speak of.

Praise be to God. Our lives can be so different now; so fulfilled and meaningful. Choices clearer, paths more defined. God, you are my glory and my everlasting love. Let me be a faithful servant unto you. For I know my life is of little consequence without you in it. Deliver me from my own ego and self-importance allowing only truth and the Christ light to shine through. Blessed are your people. Ready their hearts and minds for the word of the Lord. Glory to God. Amen

LETTER 29

*I*N SILENT PREPARATION FOR OUR Lord let us give thanks and praise without regard for the gifts that are given us daily. We may not always recognize our abundance and blessings, but let us rejoice and receive it. Give thanks this day, O children of God, and open your hearts to receive more of what I have to offer you. Is not your place in heaven of utmost importance to you? Can I not show you the way better that anyone? You have become hard-hearted and lost in the ways of the world. It is never too late to lose yourself to the love of God. Never too late to set aside the hopes and dreams of the world and pick up the desires that harbor in your heart. Forget all that you were taught of success and limitation and learn a new way of being. A way that can and will truly serve you all the days of your life. I call to you now. Lay softly upon my pallet. Lay your head upon my hands. Regret nothing you have done and lay to rest any thoughts of sadness and anger. Rest peacefully in my presence. You will move quickly toward your peace of mind, your serenity, allowing all that haunts you to be lifted up and transformed.

I have come to tell a story of how man has gone astray of the teachings taught so long ago. I came to tell how man could transform himself and thus his world around him. Misinterpretations of my words have held you back long enough. Ready yourselves for an unlimited power to unleash itself upon you giving you great strength, love and understanding, great abundance, success, and clarity. A power and a presence like no other comes. My words will be made clear. There will be no more interpretation of the word for it shall be made manifest into this world. Your feet will not touch the ground when this power overcomes you.

Be patient in the nearing days. I will not forget the promises I have made to you. Understand for now that there are many things unseen that cannot be revealed to you now. In time you will know all. Alive with wonder and excitement you will all be when my God comes forth to grace you with his power that I speak of. The heavens will open up in tribute. Trumpets will sound the glorious invitation to praise him. Children will lie down in the streets with an absolute knowing in their hearts that this is the presence of God come down to touch them. They will know long before your elders will. Look to the heavens once more and see the angels rejoicing, proud of each earth bound soul for their journey in changing the planet. For it will have succeeded in turning hate into love, fear into comfort, sadness into joy. Forgiveness and understanding will be a way of life.

Turn not away and call this foolishness but the reality we strive to attain each day. We change our molecular structure in a moment of changed thought. We can change the world in ways we never thought possible. You move swifter, quicker and with more intention than ever before. Souls are searching their purposes more that ever before. It's all happening right now. Forever will life on earth be changed and you will have been a part of it.

LETTER 30

OREVER LET THE PSALMS OF David be uttered from your lips. Praise God and honor him with your daily actions. Sing his praises to the masses allowing him to show great things through you. Forever let the words of God be inscribed on your heart. Tell all whom you meet the wonders he has performed. Thank God for his understanding and merciful heart for he judges no man. In his infinite wisdom there is only one judgment of whether you have a love in your heart for the Father. Because you are one there is no separation. Love for your brother will always be love for God and vice versa.

Live to know the Lord more intimately as he lived to show you how. To all that would give their hearts, stand tall and receive the blessings of God. For those of you who will not give your heart, stand back and watch while turmoil and anguish leave you paralyzed. Look no further than your own house for your misery for there it will lie in front of you. This will not be caused by your Father in heaven, but of your own accord. This is not vengeance, but self-actualization. There will be nothing about yourself that you will not have discovered on the hardest path of all. Your ways are not always the best ways. Leave them now and follow me.

My hope for all of mankind is that they come to the Father in haste and not live the lives of turmoil your ancestors have endured. Let us shift our consciousness now to change our reality here and our future in heaven. Place faith in the hand of God that it will be done and it will be done. I have spoken the words of love, forgiveness, peace and understanding of your brethren. I have told of your parts in this redemption. I have laid down for you a path on which to follow and shared with you some of the joys and blessings to come. Go within yourselves and feel where you might be lacking in your lives. Not monetarily but spiritually. Do you need guidance with being too judgmental? Do you harbor grudges against others? Have those that have harmed you been forgiven? Look deep within and then ask for a healing from God. Bring everything to the surface. Have you done things you haven't forgiven yourself for? Bring those to God as well and ask forgiveness. Pull it all out to make way for the light that will fill your voided rooms. Lift up your eyes to heaven and thank God for taking every hurt away from you, every pain, every lacking thing in your life. *Thank you, God, for your love and understanding of our hearts and souls.* You are surfacing from the depths and your darkest days to a life of genuine joy and happiness. Continue to give God all your burdens and trials. There is nothing that is bigger or more complex than the Lord your God.

Remember me! Remember me and all that I am.

LETTER 31

ONCE AGAIN I TELL YOU, my children, you are not alone. Keep vigilant and I will let you know the paths I have prepared for you. Each day as we communicate, your paths will become clearer and more accessible to you. All things will fall into place. Your fulfillment and desires will become realities. Your children's lives will fall into harmony. Your relationships will flourish and you will move forward with a single mindedness of purpose instead of scattered thoughts and emotions. The importance of time with me each day cannot be emphasized enough. Without the steady hand of God you are tossed on the waves like a small boat. I can calm the seas and lead you to the steady shore, but you must make the call. The daily effort is well worth it. Living more fully is but a dream to you now. Never having experienced it you don't know what it entails. I can bring you to that place of peace daily. I can show you right steps from wrong.

LETTER 32

LAVISH THE LITTLE ONES WITH love; they are so innocent. Give them a safe harbor in which to rest. There is much on them these days. Listen to them with a careful ear. Judge not; only love. When they are in need of help give it and hold no grudge. They lash out because they do not understand. Let their disrespect hurt you not. Look deeper into what you can do to relieve their anguish. They speak of very intelligent matters among their peers. Show them you think their opinions worthy and meaningful and that you'll back them no matter what.

Is that not exactly what the Father has done for you? Why do you treat your children differently? Are they less precious in God's sight?

Loosen your control as they grow and need less guidance. They will always make mistakes, only be there to hold them when they fall. How difficult it is for them to see the beauty in maturing and becoming independent. Growing and evolving just like you. Feel their warmth and love and be pleased with it, no matter how fleeting. Your children do not tarry long for they have big, important things to do—just like you.

Do you see the correlation? You are no different to your Father in heaven than your children are to you. Does God love you any less?

Save the children; they have everything to live for. Hold their hands through crises, don't condemn. Love them as the Father loves you. They need you now. Shelter them and give them food. They are what will make the difference in the world. Out of their sorrow and pain they can change the world through the love that has been shown to them. I will lead your way, now lead theirs. The confusion is too great in their minds and they cannot see clear. I ask you to gently lead them. This takes a slow hand and patient heart to softly guide and not push. They will have to make their own decisions in the end. Pray over them and give them the Spirit that has been placed upon you. Believe in your heart that you can help make a difference and you will. Spirit will always guide you in what to say and whom to speak with. Always remember to center yourself each day with the Lord first, and then go about the Lord's work. Thank God for your words of wisdom. The impact on the world will be great.

LETTER 33

*F*OREVER BE AT PEACE WITH one another. Start no offense. Your time is golden upon the earth and you must make the most and not be caught up in others' angers, for this is time consuming and is a great drain of your love for others. Your energy cannot sustain others' anger so do not allow yourselves to be consumed by it. Lend your ear, but lend not your soul. Pray with those in need and then replenish your own supply. Fill up on the things of God that you might be better prepared for the things of the world. Set in stone the beliefs I have given you so that there is no faltering from one side to another. Stand tall in your faith and allow no one to question it. Bring forth the words I have spoken. Utter the words that will bless mankind. My words are of kindness, peace and loving action, not anger, hatred and judgment. Always remind yourselves that this is who I am. Let the all of who I am express fully in your life. If this is not what you are experiencing, change the experience. I came to show man that this can be done. You have the power to change any experience in your lives by ascending your thoughts to heaven. Incorporate the ways of God into how you think and act. Realize that the power is within you to do all things. Simple are my ways; they are not complex, so do not try to make them so. Pleased am I when my children find their inner source to guide them, give them strength and light their way. Holy Spirit rests in you to fulfill a promise made years ago. Power was transferred to you to know and transcend yourselves.

Full of fear and wonderment you are lost to which direction is yours. There is a most definite purpose for each earthly soul to attain, but there are many paths possible to reach it. Do not get caught up with the complexities of the world around you, but rest in the ease of the Christ way. The will of God rings loud in your ears. Recognize that this is God and go forth in his will, not that of your own. Feed thyself the spiritual food your soul cries out for. God has sent this manna from heaven in many forms. Take notice of it all around you. He has not left you in the darkness nor will he, but has provided you truth and the lighted way. Absorb yourself in the word then state your case with those who would listen. Share the love of Christ with all you know. In doing so it wells up inside in greater abundance. Free yourself by calling upon your Father in prayer. Waste not another day. Pick up your cross and deliver the message of God to all nations and nationalities leaving no one out. Holy Spirit comes upon you now.

LETTER 34

BEAUTIFUL ARE THESE WORDS I have given unto you. Gaze upon them with a clearer understanding, taking them with you wherever you go. Let them feed and sustain your life force when you are weak. Loving-kindness enfolds you so that you may know the way; the way of the Christed life, the way I came to show you years ago. Nothing has changed, the message is still as it was then; yet you are ready to hear and act upon it now. All that I told you then I come to repeat into the minds of men. Did I not declare that all were my children of God? Did I not say these things and greater will you perform? None of this has changed. Every person on earth *is* a child of God formed out of a physical miracle. Why have you forgotten who your Father in heaven actually is? It is and always has been the Father's good pleasure to give you the desires of your heart. Many of you do not even know what those desires are. They have been left forgotten and untouched. It is time to lift the veil and undo the worldly programming. Go back to a time when money and status did not dictate your dreams. Go back and feel what it is like to dream of doing something you would love doing every day if you could. How does it feel in your heart, your soul, and your body? Is it exciting, relaxing, or joyous? Take a moment and really visualize what that would be like. This is you and I co-creating and expressing. What is holding your life back from being exactly what you want it to be? Who and what is your source? Is it God or is it man? Do you truly know?

Surrender to the Holy Spirit and let her guide you with her wisdom. Hear what she has to say on the matter and move diligently in the direction she has guided you. Can you see or even comprehend a world where each person is fulfilling their purpose and living their dream?

Love begets love and so on through the universe. Be forever one with God and at peace with that oneness. There is no better life on earth, for in that oneness all things of heaven and earth are yours. I am your provider. Seek this oneness all of your days. It can and will be shown to you.

As if we've spoken truth you must go forth in prayer to the place where no earthly form has ever tread; the nucleus of all form, energy and matter, the very center of the universe. God is the all of everything and the very center of all. Pray in his presence; with you in him and him in you. You can ask to be shown your higher vision and higher self so that you may know and quicken towards it. You are a people known for your pleadings of heaven. Begging for things you already have and waiting until it is too late to pray. Know from this day forth—ask for your gifts. Ask for your guidance, ask for discernment between God's voice and your own. The time of pleading is over. Know that whatever you ask for you will receive in accordance with your faith. If it is prosperity that you need—ask. Move beyond the God as an outer being. He is your Father forever nurturing you from within. Men walk by your side, but God is within. The same light that shone in our Lord, shines in you. Uncover it so that all can see it. In the dark any light can be seen no matter how small. The world cares not how brightly you shine, only that you shine. The impact of each light is great upon the earth and creates an ongoing effect. Each heart transformed touches another and another to infinity. Feel good knowing you are a part of it, all of you. Take your tiniest of lights to those in darkness and they will see. You do not light the day with candles and oil and so it is with the souls of earth. Because my Son was the light of the world, you can be also. He studied and experienced his divinity for 30 years before teaching and healing the multitudes, but through Spirit that blesses you, you need not wait. Spirit is my energy working through you to demonstrate healings and the words which mankind is in need to hear. Allowing that presence to work through you should be your greatest desire, for in those moments of demonstration you are complete in your oneness with God the Father, the Son and Holy Breath. Let spirit spring forth from you, O children. It is your right and your destiny. Do not be afraid of the powers that work through you. They propel you to another level; a level of pure love in which nothing you do can be touched or destroyed by human hands. The light eternal surrounds you. You are able to move from plane to plane with ease. You fly with angels and commune with them at will. What are all your earthly treasures worth when all of this is possible? All of this and more await you at the door of heaven. When heaven and earth are one, all will see and know the oneness available to them. Hallowed be the day when the Lord shall come again and show you the way home. Ascension is certain to those who know and love God. It will be the culmination of all that has transpired, a glorious pathway to the heavens of your understanding.

Now falter not in your faith, belief, and love of the

things of God. Your ways will be tried by those of lesser faith. Darkness always seeks to extinguish the light. Let it be known that scores of angels protect my followers in ways not comprehensible to you. Faith and love in me is all that is required.

LETTER 35

O NOT BE TROUBLED. THIS day is a day of hope. Do not stay in fear. I go before you. At long last you can be free of the fears that haunt you. Recognize and acknowledge the angels sent forth to protect and assist you with all that you face. Love and anguish cannot be one. They are separate in thought. You cannot love the situation you are in if you are in turmoil. Lose the disappointment that weighs you down and lift yourself up through love. Love of all people, love of the whole. Love of the situation will transform it.

Long ago in the age of ancient Egypt there grew from the desert a great mass of people who believed in the one God, the Father. Many of the Egyptian temples and tombs had been built to worship other gods and the gold was plentiful. In these days the Israelites were scolded and persecuted for their faith for this was heresy. They continued to pray and fast for their deliverance from the persecution they did face and the Lord appeared to them and said, "Your faith is strong and I have not forgotten you. It is in your faith that the men of other gods would see and understand the God of all. Cease not your prayers for soon you **will** be delivered from this place." And the Israelites did hear and were overjoyed with the hope that had been given to them that day. For in the promise came great joy and happiness to the people of Egypt.

Have not I promised you also the kingdom of heaven,

deliverance to a better place? It is at hand. Have you the faith to get there? My God is much more accepted in this day. The masses do not persecute and crucify as they did in days of old. Can you not see your way to proclaim your faith now? Who are you hiding it from? Blessed are those who love rightly. But who of you will light the world with my words? Let that man come forth hiding nothing. All things shall be given unto him.

Forget nothing I have said so that you may translate with ease every word. Travel to nations unknown. They will be your greatest challenge yet your greatest reward. Go not alone but with the faith of many who can support the energy needed in such an undertaking. Translators, guides and villagers will be needed. Document each step and trust in me. Constant prayer will be necessary. You will experience the ways of Yahweh as he taught and be humbled in the sight of God. This path is of great importance. There is more to come to explain all that you will do. Be joyous in the promise I have given you; the hope of deliverance.

Allow the Father free reign in your lives, being true to your Christ nature (That part within you that can and will be just as Jesus the Christ was and is. The unconditional love within). Loving one another is key to transformation of yourselves as well as your world. One goes with the other. How can you truly love the world and not your brother? Take up your grain and offerings and give it to one another. This is love. Be still and know it is I that creates this love, but it is you that must manifest it and make it known. For without you I have no expression, without me there is nothing to express. Together in our oneness we can do all things. Fasten about you the food and drink in which I have provided you. The journey ahead can be long and tiresome. Seek shelter in my arms. Replenish all that you need. Remember my Son is always in your house. Call upon him when in need of supply. The word is heavy and bears down on you. Relief comes when you share all that you know. Sing freely of the blessings poured upon you. Do you think my servants crazy? Why are they so filled with joy and gladness? It is the miracles that I have pre-formed in their lives, just as I will also do unto you. There is a presence that seems unnatural to men of the world because it is not understood. A presence that inhabits the bodies and souls of those who have chosen to follow me. It will seem unnatural because it is not of this world but of the spirit world. It has been invited into the hearts of my children and lies there ready to act, ready to comfort. To err will always be a part of humanness, but as spirit becomes more dominate in the lives of men, to err will fade away. Show me your sick and hard-hearted and I will show you the miracles that can be performed when Holy Sprit is invited into their hearts. Stand back those of you who would not believe and witness unto yourselves the greatness I will perform. Ask that the Spirit would come into your lives and lay heavy upon your hearts all that is needed to cleanse and forgive yourself for all wrongs, creating a new life and a new way of living. For in this Christ Spirit you are renewed to live again. All that is in the past is in the past. Make amends to those you've harmed, forgive yourself as God the Father has forgiven you and begin anew. Be grateful each day for your newfound perspective and life. Within this life is a new freedom; a freedom from anxiety, freedom from fear, because now your faith is in the Father and not in man to provide for you. Of yourself you are nothing. With your eyes upon God you are all things. Peace go with you, my young ones in God. As your days turn into years your comfort and wisdom will grow. The wisest of you will seek communion with the Father bringing more good news to the world.

And so it will continue upon this earth.

LETTER 36

*T*HERE WILL COME A TIME in each man's life when further development is needed and desired. The Lord will come upon each and every one at the precise time to urge and guide your hearts and minds to do that which pleases your soul. This is not to say all would be teachers of the word. There are many things pleasing unto you and many things will be a blessing to all of the world. It is a time to follow your heart. A time for new beginnings. Let all men who would set aside their fabricated lives and follow their hearts do so. It is in living your dreams that you truly live. I am your source and provider. Make smart decisions and then proceed with a plan. It has taken many of you years to get into the predicaments you are in. You cannot leave them overnight. Formulate a plan and stop at nothing to achieve it. Live it. Breathe it.

LETTER 37

FEELINGS GET HURT; PRIDE IS shattered when you live in a worldly state of being. Lift your consciousness to the Christed nature that can easily be obtained. There is no need to be a priest, a church elder or renowned philosopher to take on your higher self. It is available to all who seek and ask. When your brethren smite you, take on that Christ nature and show only love. Jesus loved all of man and wished them no ill will. He was saddened but never did he seek revenge. Take care and protect yourself against the evil intentions of others by constantly sending forth love, even when they have hurt you. Keep your focus on God's love radiating to all thy would be enemies. These are the words that keep and protect you. Do not falter from this path of love and forgiveness. It is freedom.

Faint hearted are my children when faced with harsh conflict. Depend on your God center to see you through. I am there with you always. Learn to use that which can deliver you once more. When the Christ came down and said "turn the other cheek" it was not for one instance but for all time. I say to you learn to love. It is not inherent in your humanness. It is a learned response. Take the time and learn it well. It instantly transforms your being to that of love and God light. How beautiful it is to see each soul, one by one, changing into light beings. Most cannot see this for themselves but the light that surrounds you becomes brighter and brighter as you love more completely all that is around you. The world will one day be illumined with this love. For we will one day look upon the earth and we will be pleased. Light will shine brightly from one side to the next. In holy jubilation the earth will be crying, "Praise you, Father, for our deliverance. Thank you God." It is of honor to lead you there, to help you in each time of need and watch you grow and become lighter exponentially. The love of God surrounds you now and always. Go forth in love this and everyday.

LETTER 38

I CANNOT STAND BY AND WATCH the hatred and judgment that infuses your lives. How are you different from the men and civilizations of old who crucified me? My silence will not suffer any longer. The things I have come to tell you let them be heard from city to city, country to country. We shall shout the love of God from mountaintop to mountaintop. Now is the time for mankind to understand completely the words of Jesus the Christ. Make no mistake, now is the time to live those words. Generation upon generation comes after you, each with clearer understanding than the one before. Quicken this process. How long must they wait as they see their elders caught up in hatred of others and still judging men by their color and nationalities? It is time to set aside your notions of who and what you think it should be. You are like children that do not know any better. The time is now to grow up and be adults. Stop acting as children. Mature in your faith and actions. Holding on to your barbaric ideas serves no one, least yourselves. You are above this, my children from heaven. Come forth to the task at hand and illuminate all prejudice and forms of slavery, whether physical or mental, let them go. Forgiveness of all persons and nationalities is key to self-fulfillment and world peace. Lend honor to yourselves by being the first to express this forgiveness. You do not have to understand why people do the horrendous things they do, only have enough faith in God and love of yourself to forgive. Sweetened will the waters of life be for doing so. You are my lifeblood, you are my children. Stay close and let no one lead you astray. If their words are not of love, their words are not of God. Take warning keeping your eyes and ears alert. There are those who would spread the words of hatred and there are many in want to hear them. That is the way of the world. Shrink not away from them, but confront their spirits with the holy anointing spirit has given unto you. Their falsehood will loom large before them.

LETTER 39

AY THE LOVE OF GOD grow stronger in you each day, the blessings overflowing. The God light and God energy within you will grow to overflowing once you have been touched by the Holy Spirit, the Holy Comforter of life. You belong not to the world around you, but to me and my Father in heaven. When you understand this, you understand life. You should not be filled with the world, but filled with the word on high. The Holy Communicator has come and knocked; now children of God open the doors to life everlasting. You have known no joy like that of oneness. The peace and comfort of knowing every step, every move, and every thought is steeped in love.

Take your steps upon the water now. I and my Father are here to hold you. You gain nothing by staying in the boat of doubt and fear. Think not about what others will think or feel about you and your actions. They have no right to judge. This is the Father who is calling you to service and none other will ever matter.

I speak to all my children at this time. Not one, not ten, not one thousand, but all. Heed my call. Your hearts have ached with the promise within you; the longing for life. You have cried out, for the misery of it has been too great. All of life, of good and just things, call out to you now. Cry out to yourselves asking for release from your mind, your bondage and cry out for *freedom*. Can you not feel what it would be like to be free? There is not another way to truly live. Ask for your gifts of the Spirit, the gifts that belong to all mankind. Relax with no thought and be blessed, for God loves the children and sent his own spirit to reside within our hearts to urge, inspire, and transcend all things we encounter. What is man if not filled with the Holy Ghost, but that of a starving child. Come eat and drink at the fountain and thirst not for knowledge and compassion. I will never be where you cannot find me, but in plain sight.

Cast out all your demons in my name and with my authority. Cast out misery, anger and doubt. Cast out the demon of unhealthy living. Take control of your life and take back who you really are. Loosen your falsehood to yourself and the world and be everything you know you can be. Shining brightly for all to see. Blossom into full bloom, radiating your beauty and giving new life to all that encircles you. Flow like a fountain overflowing with the Spirit. All of mankind needs you now, to radiate hope where there is no hope, to radiate love where there is no love and to teach forgiveness where there is little. I have given my love so that you would have the power to do all things great and small in your lives. Waste not the blood of the lamb, but take full course and responsibility for your lives.

LETTER 40

ND THE GLORY OF THE Lord is with you this day.

We are not a people of misunderstanding; it is our birthright to know and understand all that is around us. Peace be with you and your minds as you try to decipher the mysteries that are not so mysterious to the ones who know. Shaken by truth my believers seek no other comfort or advice. The Father and I are one, seeking to be one with you so that we can perform miracles in your life and the lives of all men. Open to the belief that my blessing upon you is possible and that you are worthy. Up until the day of my death my followers had no comprehension of the power they were to receive through Holy Spirit. Fear me not; I bring to you all good things in life. Lose yourself unto the Lord and be my witness. I go before you to prepare the hearts and minds of man for the message that burns in your soul. Prepare and ready yourselves for the journey by staying in constant contact with me, doing your daily duties with love, sending out my message and taking care to study these words. Rehearse and memorize, leaving no word out. Pray for peace and understanding of your mission so that you would not make any false steps. Glory, glory, glory. The time is near for all of mankind to hear and receive the words of your God. Receive unto yourselves God's good will. Receive his utmost respect and utter no falsehood against him. Allow him to love you like no other and lead you to your soul's every desire.

Henceforth you will never be the same. Your freedom is now. Begin to see life in different shades and colors. (A new perspective.) Drink in life as it is meant to be. Live life as it was meant to be lived. Hold nothing back. Let life and the love of it flow freely from you so that you may inherit more of it. Slip not into the past feelings of lack. Hold fast to your faith that we provide you with all you will ever need and more. The promise has been made. Genuine trust in God will bring you all the blessings you desire. Lay upon the altar of God your pain and remorse, all that holds you to the world and its possessions. Filter out every negative feeling and emotion and be free. Change all that is unlike the God to that of the most sacred. Believe and feel your core changed. It is done!

LETTER 41

RAIN UPON THE EARTH, EACH city and town the fire God hath breathed into you. The fire of knowledge and truth belongs to all people. Let them ask with sincerity for their holy blessing. Feel my touch in your soul, that part of your upper abdomen between ribs. Pray out loud in Spirit and see if you do not feel me there touching you, wanting to be part of you in the core of your being.

We will be victorious in the lives of our children and cause them great joy everlasting. Never having felt the touch of the Spirit, many of man's great leaders will refuse to believe such teachings as what I have proposed; that any man can be blessed with the Holy Spirit and do miracles in his own life as well as others'. This was the promise from on high at the time of my death. These things I have done and greater you will do. Did I deceive you then? Do I deceive you now? Go forth in God's name and heal the wounded in body and spirit, heal yourselves and love one another. If you do not use the fruits of the spirit they will wither on the vine. It is much simpler to keep the fruit producing than to let it die and try to sow another. Eat of the fruit that you might bear witness of it to others.

Shallow are many of this world. Ashamed they will be on our day of reckoning, when all my good children shall be called up to meet their master. Nothing can be done at this time that will change their situation. The glory of the Lord will astonish and amaze them with their mouths open wide at the sight. The Father in his grace will send to them once again the Comforter from on high to comfort them and give them knowledge. As seen in many years past your Father has blessed the multitudes. He does it now and will do it in the years to come. Look for the heavens to open up and I and the angels to descend upon the earthly plane. Taking a great inventory we will be healing the sick, calling the strong and ministering to the misinformed. Take hold of your children and love them. A period of days this will continue before all who would be called will have ascended into the heavens. Confusion will reign supreme, as millions will be left on earth. A sadness will fall upon the land, but the sun will shine once more and the confused will understand and pray: Glory to God, Glory to God on High.

Do not be amazed at the words I give to you now. It should be of no surprise. Do not be so shocked as if I had never told you of these events. Have you become so complacent and un-expectant? This is why I come to remind you of teachings from long ago. Prepare your mind for what is to come. Ready your families, for the change and shock will be great and disturbing to many. Chaos will abound for those who gave God not a thought. Stay close to family and friends in this great time. You will want to be with one another as spiritual support. Give them your love and understanding of all that is happening. They will cling to you as a safety line because you are aware. Stand strong. Clothe yourselves in white robes (clothes) and linen representing your cleansed state and oneness with the white dove of Spirit. It will not matter in heaven what clothes you wear for you will be adorned in heavenly garments. Choose well, my children, which master you will serve, that of heaven or that of earth.

LETTER 42

*L*ET THE WORDS SPEW FORTH from thy lips that they might bless all with their love and wisdom. Before you can become a master of this world you must become a master of your own. I have been teaching you how to make this so. Our divinity depends on how far into the truth we can go. Release of the old ways will help you in your search for divinity in your own life. Constant flow of God's love through you will accelerate your progress. Yesterday is gone. Let us concentrate solely on today and the differences we can make. It is not ill minded to seek out your joy in this day and this day only. It is of faith in your God that you do so.

Have faith, o children of God, that you will be delivered and that the deliverance is today. Praise with thanksgiving for this and all things great and small. For what I have done for one, I will gladly do for another. Lest you ask, you are forgotten (passed over). In this time of great seriousness let us not forget to ask for our every need. It is in the believing, when we ask, that we receive.

In readying yourselves for the crucifixion of self do not tarry, but with quickness let it be done and gone from you. At once take up and be filled with your God self (God nature). The Spirit will fill you with all that you need; knowledge, wisdom, and understanding of which path is for you. Each step will appear clearly before you as if placed there long ago. Beauty and peace will illumine your faces so that all who know you will see God's light in you. Of foremost importance is your ability and will to shed the carnal self, the self of indulgence, the self of importance, and the self of needing all things now. How well can you do these things that I ask? Success in these areas opens you to the success I am able to give you. Without guilt, forgive yourself for mistakes of greed or egotism. Without guilt, move forward in your life to joy. Be pleased with the many changes happening to you and let it be known.

I urge you never to give more teachings than one person is ready to receive, but give them their fill and move on. You will be refused by some to share your enlightenment. Take no offense, but move on. They will be readied at a later time. Horde not the feelings and miracles, which I have given you, but share freely and without hesitation. In the inner chambers of your soul I dwell, giving you strength, comfort, and resolve. I await your call to express freely in your life. I have given you free reign, it is now my time to be able to completely express through you, taking you to heights never imagined. I cannot do so without your permission and will.

"Take me, Father, take me. Use me as an instrument of your will. Cause me to remember who it is I truly am—a child of God inherent to your kingdom and all that it entails. Use me as a catalyst for your love. Into the abyss I will fall only to be swept back up to the top of the mountain. My heart I give to you so that men may know it is for God that I stand. Lavish me with your gifts and blessings. Show me how I can better serve you today, that heaven may not seem so far away." Praise be to the Father.

Allow my works to express in you so that all of man can be blessed.

> *Glory to God, Glory to God*
> *You are my Savior, my redeemer, my everlasting*
> *love. You are my everything, you are my Lord.*
> *You are, you are my Savior*
> *You are my Savior*
> *You are my Lord.*

LETTER 43

I LONG TO SEE HAPPINESS ON each and every face. A peacefulness that transcends life. A joyfulness that can be heard around the world. Let not the things of this world keep you from your joy and I say it again, lose yourself to the love of God. He is your source, in all things. You must know this or all is lost. Your vocation is not your source. Your parents are not your source. Look with eyes of discernment and tell me whence your blessings come.

Pay attention to the everyday miracles in your life. Miracles of kindness, miracles of prosperity, miracles of love. Have you become so hardened that you cannot see? Overcome this attitude of survival that you have taken upon yourselves. The shell you use for protection is the same shell that holds you prisoner. Your ego and self-importance has you so tied to the ground you cannot lift your heads to see the light. You should be flying on the wings of angels, not groveling in the dust of mankind. I sent the Christ to lift you up and dust you off so that you could see clearly. In our universe there is a time for all things and I say to you now is the time to know and understand all that my Son came to teach. Love, forgiveness, joy in self and God. Step up and be counted, know your importance, for your God would have it no other way.

A message to all comes this day. You wait for a sign, a message to come. Make no mistake; I come to you now.

This is your message and your calling. Wait no more, but move forth in God who has prepared your way and will not forsake you. Have no fear of the unknown; embrace the newness of your life and circumstances. Give yourself freedom by allowing God to take over for you now. You have held onto your burdens long enough. It is time to let them go. Rest in my arms, let me hold and sustain you all the days of your life. You never have to go back to the same way of being. You have that choice to make now, whether or not you allow God's love and light to run your life or if you like your life just the way it is, run by all the outer circumstances. We realize it is easier said than done, but it all starts with prayer and then release.

Prayer of Release

Father, I of myself am nothing without your gentle touch and care of my soul. Take from me all of my sorrows and burdens. Fill me with thy loving spirit that I may live joyously and be filled with your wonder. In your gentle arms I lay all that binds me.

LETTER 44

EELING WEAK AND ALONE WITH God, I began to write. Write of his love, his grace, forgiveness and understanding. The feelings of peace and love are overwhelming. Words cannot describe. Spirit takes over mind and body showing me just how gentle and loving she can be. There is a certain light-headedness that always accompanies this touch from God. The words come slowly at times and at other times so quickly that I can barely write them down.

Is it not the right of each and every individual upon this earth to have all the gifts and miracles that their Father in heaven has promised them? Why have we not reached our fullest potential? There is no one special among us that has anything that we ourselves cannot achieve through the Christ consciousness already within us . . . and therein lies the answer. We must tap into that God self, the Christed nature that is within all of us, inherent by the nature of who we are. No formulas, no magic, just simple adjuration to the principles, the universal laws, laid down upon the earth through the ages.

God want you to receive a full and blessed life. Completely connected to the source of all things. A life altering experience awaits each and every soul upon this earth. The call is now. Listen and adhere to the words. We will know that it is God the Father who speaks. Prepare yourselves for all he has to give you.

LETTER 45

*W*HEN WILL I SEE THE glory upon the face of heaven for which my people long? It is of little conse-quence to you now, but pay attention in days to come. I want each and every one of you to look upon the heavens and feel a peace that is being prepared for you. A place of unexplainable comfort in which you will never want to be without. This peace I speak of will stay with you to com-fort and assist you. Hold strong to the ideas of a new day in which everyman will understand his brethren because he wants to understand. Hate and anger will fall away in the face of love pouring out from you. There is no easy road from where you are now to this time of peace I speak of. Only know it is forthcoming to you and your children after you. Your generation now is opening the gateway to this divine idea, the divine idea of a new generation com-pletely one with the God. As each of you embrace these teachings, a global change occurs. One by one the earth is transformed to a place of peace. Your children will adopt these practices of love and forgiveness readily because of the groundwork you are performing now. Be grateful for your open minds and kind hearts. It is not always easy in your everyday lives, but I know in the core of yourselves you long to connect at a deeper level with a God of your understanding and the people around you. Be in me and I in you. Make your connection by spreading God's love to all that you come in contact with. Your eyes do not even meet one another's as it is now. Make the effort to connect with all of God's children. They will begin to notice and then they will grasp and understand for themselves. Focus on those things that are right and true for all. Always help one another. Whenever in prayer ask how you can be of service to the whole that day. Most will hear and do nothing, thinking it their own voice they hear. I will always tell you what needs to be done. Trust in yourself that you hear me clearly. Forget your mind's idle chatter and allow me to shine forth. Let us go unto the hills and mountaintops waiting for your new self to emerge. Do you doubt this miracle can occur?

I will show you many miracles in your own lives. Cry out to the heavens when you are ready to receive my love. I will come upon you in accordance with your faith and bless you with a mighty awakening, lifting your heart and mind into the heavens that you may stay and commune there with the angels. This is where all of wisdom lies. This is where all of creativity, creation and inspiration harbor until found. Once you have found this incredible place, you will yearn for its presence every moment of every day, to be a constant in your life. Making right choices and decisions for you, this heavenly place will be part of you. Once again, heaven on earth, here . . . inside, the largest part of who you are becoming. With God as your the creator, co-creating a life with you, how could any of his inspiration and creativity be wrong? Tap into this heavenly source that will enrich your lives beyond measure. It would be foolish once you know of it, to do anything of importance without it. Why would you not consult the heavens and ask for divine guidance, that you would never have to struggle again?

All things in a new perspective, your body and soul evolve further into a oneness with God. There will come a time when there will be no separation. No separation from God, no separation of class, gender, race or religion. We are one in Spirit; let us be one in love.

Truth is hard to find when every interpretation of my word is different. This is why I say it is so important for every man to find his own truth in the words I have given him. Take what information you have and be discerning according to the needs in your own life, not others. Ask for wisdom and guidance and I will see you through. What is truth for you cannot be truth for another. If one man seeks to burn incense and another would don robes of gold, it is that man's prerogative to do so if that is what creates or amplifies his connection with the creator. I do not request any of these rituals, but I do not condemn them either, nor should you. Let us only share the truth of what we know and let all others absorb what they can and will. We should do no more. There will be those among you who will thirst and ask questions, wanting the knowledge you have been given, all to make a difference of great magnitude in their own lives. Do not hold back, but share all that you know for as long as you are able. There will also be those that want nothing of it. Protect yourselves and be not offended. They have not reached that time in their lives of thirsting for the word. They have not been prepared.

Today is a glorious day . . . a day of recognition of our God . . . a day of harmony and right thinking. We no longer are in need of the trappings that held us. With joy we lift all to God for in the love of God there is no sacrifice, only joy. There is much to say on the matter of giving. It is the giving of self that matters most; giving over to God your thoughts and actions and allowing him to fill you with great intentions and purpose. It has never been easy for man to achieve this. In his mind are all the reasons why he cannot give all of himself to God. There are debts, children, and spouses that all take precedence. Do you see how this is backwards from what God intended? If you put God first, there is no way he would not provide one hundred fold for your children, spouse and debts. Your "things" have a different energy around them and some are not of importance in your walk with God. Recognize this to be true as you walk through your own life. Ask, "What 'things' do I have that are ego-driven?" It does not mean you cannot have great things if you follow God, only look at your intention behind all that you have. Is the car you own because you love the way it feels, or is it intended for your friends to see and notice? Be aware as you go through your day and try to recognize and lose your ego as you notice it. Follow your instincts when making new decisions and be completely honest with yourselves. It is the wish of all the heavens for you to have your every desire and there is a point in which every person can become unattached to all earthly things and still enjoy every one of them. It is a growth process that must be taken with care. Allow me to show you the steps and together we can be free.

STEPS TO CO-CREATING

Have you ever felt alone even when surrounded by people? Have you been placating others, allowing them to think you are something different than you truly are? In co-creating we must find and get to the "what of who" you really are so that it may shine abundantly to the world.

Then, because you will be in complete harmony, the world will respond to you differently and it begins with your 1st step of love.

Love of others is always easier than love of self so lets begin with self. Step one—Wanting to make a difference in the lives of others you give freely to everyone because it changes you at a core level. By giving and sharing love, you begin to love yourself. The loneliness within disappears because now you have purpose and a divine mission. It no longer matters what people think of you. In your mind and heart you are doing something that matters. I ask you to find a foundation, charity, church or community to give of yourself. It never matters where. It may be next door. The point is to give of self.

Step two—start forgiving those who you feel have harmed you. In their lives they are on a journey all their own and not any easier than yours. Forgive them that you may move on to a richer more fulfilled life. Forgive family and friends . . . people of your past. We are not asking you to forgive what they have done to you, but forgive them as fellow humans, fellow souls, living at the only level they know to live. In forgiving them you raise the level of who you are exponentially. Most importantly in this step, you must forgive yourself so that you can love yourself and all others.

Step three—give of life's flow. In giving you receive back multiplied. As you live in God's presence and his love begins to flow from you, so does love flow to you. As prosperity flows from you, so does it flow to you multiplied. Give in joy and happiness for all you have in your life and all that you know you will receive because this is the law of life.

Step four—peace and harmony must be a daily part of your life. This is only found through Holy Communion with God. This precious time is not to be forgotten for within it lies your every question answered, your every problem solved. In his presence you receive your peace and harmony that will stay with you throughout the day. Ask for what it is that you need and it shall be given. The wisdom of the ages abides there and who of you does not need that clarity of life? Breathe in the silent spirit that surrounds you in these moments of prayer and mediation. You will find the "what of who you are" there; that you may know and let it express forth into the world to glorify God and self.

Step five—have gratitude for all things great and small not only in your own lives, but also in the world and the lives of others. Have gratitude for the beautiful skies, the forests and streams, mountains and green valleys. All of our abundance comes from God; let you not forget to have appreciation for those blessings. When have we of our humanness ever created such beauty? In our thankfulness we receive a gracious heart. A heart filled with compassion and gratitude.

Step six—take inventory of your life and dispose of those things that drain you of life's precious energy. Dispose of those things that do not serve you, but serve the world. Clear your house and yourself of unclean thoughts and behaviors. Make the conscious effort to eliminate fears and sorrows. Sweep your body and mind of the envy and resentments that can harbor there. Only by the power within and trusting in God can it be done. Believe in me now and let not the darkness return for I am the giver of light eternal. Waste not away on the fears of tomorrow, but let me guide you fearlessly along the way.

Step seven–lay upon the altar of heaven your ego and self-righteousness. There is no room for the light of God and your selfishness. Be the light, not just mere man. Whosoever is for me, who can be against them. In your everyday lives let you glorify God before glorifying yourselves. Do not sit in the throne of self-righteousness, but step down freeing yourselves.

There will be a time when all is understood; it is not yet come. These are the words of the Father that you might begin to comprehend your purpose and meaning. Hasten your oneness with God through these steps to the kingdom of heaven. Lay before me all that I would not ask for. Be blessed, young children of God . . . be blessed.

LETTER 46

*F*ORSAKEN ARE YOU, MY BELOVED ones, that cannot see your way to put your sights upon heaven. I have given you every due course in which to follow. What more shall I say? It is not a road of difficulty but one of concentration. You must be aware at all times of your thinking and your actions. Be tenacious with yourselves, never losing sight of your God self. Prayer and meditation will assist you in these areas. They are simple steps to follow. Don't make them more difficult than they are.

Feign softly, your gentle heart knows no peace. When you are alone, place your hands in the hands of the Christed one and there find your solace and understanding. Peace emanates to you. Rest beneath my comforting shelter. Let my warmth and love fill your senses to overflowing. The difficulties can be over if you choose. Find your way into the arms of heaven letting love shine forth as it was meant to, emulating the Christed one. You long to walk in the footsteps and be a master just as he was. The seed is within each one of you. How can you say that you are participating in life and not help the seed that is within you grow? Take control, through concentration, and lose control all at once. Through faith, and not doing as man would bid, you can reach your fullest potential, but remember, the seed must splinter before it grows. The misery from whence many of you come crawling is unnecessary. Only after admitting complete failure in managing your own lives do you reach for the hand of God. Here your spiritual experience begins for you have learned first hand that you are not capable of yourself to conquer matter. (That which presents itself to be overcome daily in your lives.) The refuse of life you consciously and unconsciously create. Protect yourselves from the storms by knowing and keeping your truth close at hand. The winds toil at times, but the hand of truth never falters. Be steadfast in your beliefs and the Father will see you safely to your shore. Live in light and the blessings at hand. Your presence is greatly needed upon this earth. Forever light the way of lost and forgotten souls. Let this be your mission upon the earth. Be faithful and of good cheer; your faces to illumine the night.

LETTER 47

*W*HEN THE PHILISTINES CAME UPON the land they destroyed many villages and leaders. They had hardness in their hearts for all who were unlike them. Those that worshiped a god different from theirs ran the risk of being exiled or killed and many a people perished at the hand of the Philistines.

The arguing has not ceased for a thousand years. It is and never shall be a man's place to judge another man and how he worships. Cut thy tongue before you speak such heresy. God in heaven wants all to know and recognize him, but he never wishes war upon your brethren. He never wishes judgment. He will make all of those decisions in due time; he does not lay that burden on man. He asks that you all speak truth, but if one man hears and does not agree, move on. The man will know and understand in time his own truth. You've made a difference already just by speaking what you know to be true for you. Judgment will never be a part of God's message for you to take. Step down from the throne of God and let God be judge. Your most valuable asset is to be at the right hand of God, to be his good servant that he may use you to perform his deeds to the glory of heaven and earth. It is an honor to be of God and have him with you at every moment. It is a blessing not to be forgotten.

Change your hardened hearts to exclude no one from a loving, Christ-filled heart. Make every man equal in your sight. Love them all the same. It is much harder to love an angry man than a loving one, but the difference you can make will be much greater. Stand side by side as brothers, sharing cultures and history; shut the door on no one. You may not agree with their beliefs and philosophies, however, love transcends all. Learn the languages and ancient dialects so that you may communicate freely with one another. Be not shallow minded and stubborn. You have been ego driven and selfish with your riches and economic gain, while the world around you starves. Is there no wonder there is hatred on this earth? Share of yourselves and feed those hungry to learn what you know, do not share your ammunition to liberate them. It does not make it right now or ever, but let this be a call to action, to sharing and loving those that are different from you. Self-righteousness has never served you well. Gather up the wounded and show them love and mercy. It is a difficult time for all. War is never right. There is no place for hatred in a world striving for peace. Only after there has been too much death and too much heartache and the realization that no one has truly won, will it come to an end. Why must man always come to this in the name of God and self-righteousness? The hearts of man can be changed in other ways. Yes, we believe that each soul should have the freedom to worship their God in anyway they choose, as long as they hurt no one due to their traditions and beliefs. Let us not impart our opinions on them, but let God do the workings needed in their lives. By example we show our faith and love for all people.

LETTER 48

*Y*OUR CHRISTED FORM TRANSCENDS ALL matter. Bring yourself to that higher plane and begin to understand the inner workings of time, space, and matter. One of the gifts we have been given is to take whatever situation or false forms is presented to us and transform it for good. The power that has been given to us, in spirit, is more than enough to rise above all difficulty, real or perceived. Matter is no different and can be transformed in equal measure to our understanding and consciousness of it. To understand fully our positioning within the all of everything, the entire universe, we must first learn to understand our relation to all things within our own world. Trapped in our finite minds it is difficult to understand so we must expand our way of thinking. Of our own power we cannot achieve this higher mind consciousness, but must ask for assistance from on high, whatever we choose to relate to such as Holy Spirit, the holy breath, angels from on high, that energy is the only one that can bring us to that higher consciousness where we are able to transcend all that may confront or hinder us.

Jesus Christ was the ultimate master of matter. Through his miracles and healing work he demonstrated God's power within himself. No matter how insurmountable the circumstance, it mattered not, because he was filled to overflowing with the Spirit. The same Spirit that he left for each and every one of us here on earth. To find that power within we must put all other things aside and focus solely on God energy and how it is entwined molecularly within all things. If you can change self through God love and God energy, can you not transform any problem or ill will? Moving forward to prosperity and abundance manifestation and further still to objects of substance.

Water, earth, and fire are all elements charged at a different frequency that can be tapped into once given the gateway to that higher awareness. To heal the wounded and feed the masses is our birthright through the love that God has shown us. To part the oceans and walk on water, these are but a fragment of what you will do. It is not saved for only those of scientific minds, but for all to discover and create miracles in their own lives. However great or small the challenge may be, use all that you have available to you. Why go through suffering if there is a better way? Our God has given us power freely; let us learn to use it. The challenge is not whether God has provided enough to do all that you long to do, but have you provided God with all he needs to do it with?

LETTER 49

THE SIMPLICITY OF A GOD-FILLED life is astounding. There are no scientific formulas or codes. You have been given all the instruction you need, only decide to act upon them. They are not as difficult to learn and understand as you think; they only take a conscious decision. Deciding to do what's right and trusting you will be taken care of for it. Your joy in life multiplies by the amount of effort you place in serving the whole of mankind. Look no further than yourself for that happiness you seek. Forsake all other ways to follow in the footsteps of right. You will watch in amazement as the blessings start to flow to you. The modern-day miracles do exist and will take place before your eyes as you make that commitment to love and serve the higher calling and not man. Lost time is of no consequence. It matters not how long or how far away you have been from the light. The only thing that matters now is your decision to give yourself to God at this moment, resting yourself and your soul in his loving, comforting arms. Let him handle the miracles you need in your lives today. You are special and extremely valuable to the heavens no matter what you've done or what road you've traveled. Be of one mind with the Father who loves you. Ask for clear guidance on which direction you are to go now that you have the hand of heaven to lead the way.

Lavish yourself with kind words . . . you are all in need of them. Pray that all men would take these steps of faith so that all men could be in Christ consciousness and thus the world would be of one mind, the God mind. You think it is done according to his will? Look upon who rules the earth now; it is man's will that conquers and destroys at this time. As long as human will is in control it continues in this cycle. All of man must surrender to bring about peace. War will not be the answer to that which you seek. Only through tolerance and love can you bring about peace. Graduate from your infancy of understanding. Move forward to the greater good of all. Lay down your swords of righteousness and pick up you the scythes of justice. Cower not, but neither should you oppress the nations with condemnation. Ask in earnest what it is they seek from you. How can you help them and is there any place for forgiveness in their hearts for any man other than themselves? What has been your offense and how can it be rectified? How can you do better in the future? Pride is important in small doses; to be humble and of good service to others is more important. Fervent prayer is needed so that all people of all nations might see the need for these actions and words of peace. Let us hold vigil to the quest, in honor of those gone before. They want this peace with all their hearts for the entire world. Let not their lives be in vain, but have everlasting meaning.

Converge upon the world with this message of peace, tolerance, and love to bring about a higher level of living for all. Closer to heaven are thee, those who follow the Lord. Align yourselves with God and all will become clear. The why's, the how's, and the why not's will fade away. Crystal images will appear before you to explain all that you have ever longed to know. Beautiful faces of angels will appear and speak to you and make their presence known. My guides will give you information needed to begin and complete your personal missions. These are the gifts of God in which your connection to him is imperative to receive them.

Truth continues to flow to you daily. It did not end when Jesus ascended, it only began. He gave us the way and the truth while he lived, but promised that through the Holy Spirit we would continue to be fed the truth and be shown the way even more so than when he was alive. The Bible is precious and is filled with the words of God, but there is so much more to learn that we are being given every day. My children, thousands of years of living have gone by, do you think your Father in heaven lay dormant? All that is has been said and done? I am the living God who speaks truth to all who would listen. I am the culmination of all that has been and ever will be. I am the bearer of fruit in your lives and I have not forsaken you for 2000 years. I am with you always, only listen and know that I am gently guiding, prodding, and nurturing, bringing you into a closer connection with me. I give you truths and understandings and it is not I alone who does this, but all of heaven. Awaken from your earthen sleep and tap into your spiritual side so that you can know and coincide the two worlds in harmony. Be on the earth, but not of it. Keep your hearts and minds ever in the heavens with no anchor tying your spirit to that of the world. I am the giver of light and life everlasting.

Young hearts lay bleeding at my feet, crying out for hope and understanding. Weak and alone they shiver in uncertainty. This is not the life they'd imagined or dared dream of. Turmoil and gut wrenching, life has taken them hostage and the pain is too great to bear. In desperation they call forth death, for it is better than living. My angels, go to them and hold their hands so that they can know what love feels like. In their transition hold them in your arms that Spirit might comfort them and lay them to rest, with peace.

LETTER 50

*S*TATIONARY AND FULL OF COMPLACENCY are the people of little faith. Just enough knowledge to condemn others, but not enough to help themselves. It is in their quiet moments of frustration that I call. Feel the joy that the gentle touch of heaven gives to you when you respond to its call. Feel the slowly falling tears of happiness that awe and inspire you. Feel the gentle hand of God that touches you. Feel in all your humanness that I am with you always and should you seek for more, only ask. It is the asking that opens the door to your heart. I will respond in waves of love and you will know without a shadow of a doubt that I am your God brought to you through the Spirit; living, breathing, and manifesting through you.

Beauty is your name, o' Lord, that we of human suffering would be allowed to live in your grace. All that we have been through has been forgotten. I am of little consequence without you in my life. Let your love and compassion flow freely from me now.

Since the beginning of all beginnings, God's immortal being has been. Through thousands of years of darkness the energy existed, expanding from the universe to infinity without limit or confinement. The omnipotent force and energy sought outer expression and clear form to completely evolve. A world full of light and love was created with no detail being forgotten. A world of beauty and wonder fully expressed. Think of its perfection as a self-sustaining life form. It has never been in need of man for its existence yet it gives freely to man and all his needs. The miracle of God's love.

Rectify man's way and preserve the life force which sustains you. You are a deadening drain upon its resources. Wake and see, pray for balance and harmony within your ecosystems. Pray that man would tread lightly upon its lands, taking little and leaving much, providing for generations to come. Drought and pestilence are forthcoming lest you conserve the land and in collective prayer change the face of earth with loving action. Join together in movement to support one another's thought processes in visualizing and asking for an abundance of natural resources and environmental change to facilitate that. What you collectively believe becomes the reality in which you face. Elementary laws have not made it into the mainstreams of society. It is time to take loving action to change the world in which you live. The power of God can do all things, but first the channel must be opened in you through asking. How do you ask? Through prayer. Allow the abundance of heaven to rain down upon the earth that all living things might prosper.

LETTER 51

$\mathscr{I}$N THE YEARS BEFORE CHRIST there was among the earth a great awakening of such magnitude that has not been seen before or since. A realization of things to come as they were prophesied in days of old. The earth made ready for the coming of the Lord Jesus Christ. It was spoken about in streets and kingdoms long before the event occurred. Such is the time now. A time of re-awakening, of knowing that all that was prophesied will come true. Speak of it throughout the lands. It is no secret that Josea comes once more to his people home, ascending into the heavens upon chariots of fire. Many who have gone before will re-appear and be part of the glorious event. Three days and three nights will it continue, the greatest gifts of all to fall down upon the earth. Complete clarity and understanding with the knowledge of the ages to supersede all that has been known before. There will be nothing to fear for those who know the truth for they will have expected this event to take place and will know it is their God, the one God, who opens the heavens to receive his beloved ones. Had I not sent a messenger to foretell all that comes and will occur there would have been much chaos and uprising. There will be plenty as it is for there will be thousands in confusion. They are not forgotten but will have more trials to overcome, as they will be on the earth during a most difficult time. They are not alone, for many of God's children will stay behind because it is their calling to guide the blinded ones home. Let them ever keep their faces towards heaven. This will see them through. In the distance there is hope of a brighter day. A day unlike cause and effect, but that of pure form. Immediate manifestation. Light beings predominantly upon the earth plane. Light form connecting with light form to create faster and higher energy patterns floating from one plane to another effortlessly exactly as the master Jesus did after his ascensions into heaven. He came upon the earth many times in form, as man, not ghost; and so shall you.

Welcome this re-awakening of this new time spoken about since days of old. It is not of new thought; it is the realization and manifestation of truths spoken long ago. Embrace them into your consciousness so that you would not be afraid nor left behind. Your bodies will falter under the test of time, but your souls will live on forever. Lift up thine eyes and hearts to the heavens; it is I that dwells with you there.

Feast upon all that I have given you and all that is to come. Pour my blessings upon you now. Take oath and go serve with the utmost integrity, sincerity and love. Your place among angels has been set aside. Thank the heavens for your clarity of purpose and divine intervention of your soul. Begin to see yourself in the holy light as I see you in total perfection. As this perfect child you are to walk and talk with my guidance within you, every step of the way. My heart breaks with your common dissatisfactions when there is so much to be joyous about. So much has been given to you already that you refuse to see. How great are the gifts to mankind that they have no perceived use for. I offer you sustaining life and yet you choose not to accept it.

Weary are the faces of mankind as they look to the

future. Hope is not lost; take to the streets a message of hope eternal. Those who would let you ban together, for there is strength and love in your numbers. Portray the love that your God has for all of his children. Call upon the Spirit to intervene and heal the sick. Exude love and you my children, will be that ray of hope the world needs. Group together I say, with prayer and support for one another and all of mankind. Judgment and self-righteousness has no place here. One group shall not shun another, but with open arms embrace the knowing that the mission holds true and is ultimately the same, bringing peace, tolerance and understanding to all. Work together in harmony to bring good to the world. Validate and bring forth witness to the miracles you will perform in my name. Ask for deliverance from all that has oppressed you and with clear movement seek to save others of the same oppressions. Long-lasting effects will change nations forever.

At the end of days a mighty wave will come across the land, symbolic of its cleansing.

LETTER 52

THE ANGELIC MESSAGE

SOFTEN YOUR BROW AND DO not be angry. There is only love for you here. You ask why in confusion and frustration yet your heart knows why. Listen to it carefully. God does not attack you or wish harm upon you, but your angels are here to guide you ever so gently through this difficult time to the right path. We allow you your many tangents, however there comes a time we must stop you and redirect you.

Do not be attached to material things. It is time to release. We realize there are many circumstances that we affect. We save you from many situations and co-create others, all for the good of the whole. Remember our purpose is not to collect trophies, but to shine God's light more abundantly throughout the world.

LETTER 53

*P*LANT YOUR FEET FIRMLY ON the ground yet keep your heart in heaven. In doing so you will be able to connect with both worlds and live joyously in doing so. Enjoy all that is around you—the soft summer rain, the raging rivers, and mists rising from mountaintops. I am easily found in nature. If that is your only avenue to the Father then go there, but remember, I am also in the boardrooms and corporate buildings, the construction sites and living rooms. Find me there as well. Do not miss out on your opportunity of love and guidance throughout your day. I am constant. I am the same wherever you find me.

These gifts of life I have given unto you are most precious. Be gentle and loving with yourselves. By staying connected to your source you will innately know how to comfort yourselves and others. It comes in fleeting thoughts and ideas. Place yourself among all others and know you are most worthy of God's love and your own self-love. The seed, which was planted within you, has not yet blossomed. You must nourish it and continue to fertilize the soil in which it lies. Within your chemical make up is a trusting, reliable, pure and loving, light filled human being with God energy at your core. All come into this world with these qualities and then quickly adapt to their individual surroundings creating separate person-alities and defense mechanisms to safeguard themselves from hurt. No matter how small the pain, to a beautiful new child it is tremendous. The walls of defense come up and the trusting, pure and loving light begins to fade and become like all the others, until the seed begins to sprout and seeing the sun once more, begins to grow stronger. Reaching towards the light the soul (or seed) is no longer in the dark and with full clarity and knowledge of exactly what it is to do, the soul goes out into the world to fully express his God self and soul's purpose. Individualized once more, the human spirit has attained freedom. Freedom from pain and freedom from darkness.

Do not mistake my words for idle chatter. Words you have heard, yet heed not. It is my wish for all of you upon the earth to find the peace and clarity I speak of. To live a most complete and passionate life. To love the experience of living. I tell you all I know to tell you and yet you want more. Dear children, ask and it shall be given unto you. All knowledge is available to you when you connect to a higher realm. It can always be attained through prayer and meditation. Be tenacious in your prayer life; it is the key to understanding. A passionate, God-filled life is available to everyone who seeks to walk in oneness. Come unto me. Come unto me all that seek this life and be blessed with Holy Spirit.

LETTER 54

*A*LLOW MY LOVE TO FLOW freely from you. A beacon in the night to calm the storms of life. Believe I am with you always.

It is pleasing to the Lord to see his children ascending their thoughts to heaven. Making their choice to follow God in every situation whether in the raging storm or the serene calm. There is not one thing that I would not give unto you. Open your hearts that all of my blessings may flow to you. Victory is mine that I might glory in it for a time. I have not spoken from an ill or dark place but from a place of God's glory and everlasting love. Fill the basins with holy oil and anoint each living soul of Christ. An outward sign of protection against all that may curse and offend thee. Take no pleasure in fighting the wars, internal or external, but delight in the feeling and desire for peace that I have given to you through this anointing of oil. You need very little in the way of things; it has all been supplied for you. It is not long before I present myself to you once more. I am the night prowler who will steal away with his beloved in the blink of an eye. I come to carry you home, rely on my strength and insight. Follow my way so that there is no question or doubt in your mind as for whom you stand. There should never be a question.

Forgive my inadequacies to open your hearts while on earth in human form. What were the words that may have shown more light and healed more sick? I wept for the unknowing of what to say and asked my Father, "What shall I say, what shall I do?" I gave all that was within me to give and man did not understand and spat at my feet, for the ground that I walked upon I was not fit to walk. Such hatred in their eyes. I had to rise above that I would fulfill the promise made by my Father in heaven. As I looked out over the people I could see every angel, every spark of light that was there supporting me on my journey and my destiny. I write to you now, as it is another opportunity for man to lift higher. Allow me entrance into your hearts. I come in earnest that you may know the way unto the Father. I want to personally touch each and every one that you would feel the joy, feel the happiness I have to give you. I see each light and I see the darkness. I come to bring the light in greater measure that all might see with clarity.

Seek not those things of the world, but seek me first and the kingdom is yours. While I am still here let me speak to you of anger and rage. Nothing but death to your inner most being occurs when you are in rage. You all must learn to control it. It dampens the spirit within you, not another. Bring harmony to yourself in every hostile situation through immediate prayer, praying for calm, love and understanding of the situation. The stresses upon your body and your soul are great and your light diminishes to almost nothing. This must be controlled. As Christ beings, the children of God, it is your duty. In doing so you fulfill a part of your soul's purpose. Hand away your control so that I can bring peace. It is never easy for the children of God to follow my ways and not their own. As you have turned your back on the Garden of Eden, that oneness was taken away. Turn around once more, the door to the

Garden is open and will receive you into its comforting arms.

Can one function in two places at once? In The One-ness of the Garden and the separation of the earthly plane? I say yes with all the conviction of the angels. Your feet will be firmly upon the earth but your soul will be that of heavenly grace experiencing a consciousness bigger than anything you can imagine. Words do not describe the magnitude of all there is. I have fed you one piece at a time and as your consciousness expands and grows I will fill you with more.

I have seen the barren lands and the people that abide there. You will touch them, not with your hands, but mine—giving life to them. I am the healer of nations and I go with you in full glory. Do not plan and debate all that must go on or be done. If you truly believe I provide all, I will provide it before you know your need of it. Glory, glory to God this day.

LETTER 55

AM THE SON OF GOD . . . lead me to your highest council that I may bring justice and deliverance to them for their wrong doing. I speak in simple terms and yet who will listen? It is not a message to the ignorant or well educated, it is a message of peace to all people. Mirror your image upon my own. Take up the armor of God and press on. Those who have sat passively by, this is your call to action. Spring forth a new person; astound the world with your willingness and might. Yesterday will forever be in the past; begin a new day now. Stand your ground and shield your beliefs from those who would steal them away. Quietly, subtly they begin placing doubt within your hearts. With a most thunderous voice proclaim who you are and who your God is. Let it be known that you are a Christ child. Because you believe that I died on the cross, because you believe that I am Son of God and because you believe that I resurrected and came again to earth, these things you will do also. All of this and nothing short of this brings to you the glories of heaven.

Poised and ready my children await the futile wars of earth to cease. There can be no peace until a resolution is met through constant open communication and a willingness to understand all points of view. A love of all people must be present for such an event to occur. Bring peace in your daily lives and it will bring peace into the world. Whatever you do today, comes back to bless or curse the earth in good measure. Know this to be true.

HEARING THE VOICE OF God

LETTER 56

A MESSAGE TO MY PEOPLE AND the world . . .
Open your ears as well as your hearts this day all children of God and hear the message of peace I bring forth. Join thy hands together regardless of nation. Regardless of color or age. Join together in sanctimony and release all judgment one for another. Look to the heavens this day and ask for the ability to forgive all who have harmed you. It is this day that the heavens hold dear for this is the day all consciousness shifted. This is the day all humankind changed from merely existing to feeling their feelings and knowing that they were alive because so many had died. All of you let love pour from you to your brothers and sisters in the world. Let it cross the oceans and radiate the distant shores. It is time to remove yourselves from your little world and view yourself and the world in a greater light. See a greater vision of peace and know that it is possible. Reach out respectfully and connect with others around you. Reach out to those in foreign lands. Teach peace and tolerance to your young ones. Show love and they will know no other way. Allow me to use you as my vehicles to world peace and let us put this pain behind you. As in every situation you will move forward, but move upward as well. Do not forget to shine the love of God outward into the world, always looking up from whence it comes.

How can I use you who seem to be of little importance to man? Remember your ways are not my ways. You are of great importance, each and everyone, to the heavens. Let it flow forth from you that which Holy Spirit will give you in perfect time. Raise your hands and proclaim that which will be given unto you. Hold nothing back. The ones in need of it will be guided to hear. Worry not; if you speak to just one man it is better than not speaking at all. Have faith in God. Have that unwavering, complete faith that knows all is well and that each of you are completely supported and taken care of. Have faith that God's power can overcome all difficulties facing nations and facing you individually. Watch as ivory towers fall and monarchies crumble. Peace is all that will be tolerated from a people in pain and grieving around the world. Position yourselves as beacons of light to others in fear. They will need you now. Be at complete peace. Miracles happen no matter what the circumstance. Individuals and groups alike will come to know God on a personal level through these miracles that God's children will perform. Quicken your hearts and minds to the knowledge that this will happen as it should.

Holy Spirit, through your hands, will perform amazing things. God wants you to have these gifts and wants you to use them. In his infinite mercy he touches us and makes us whole. Let us glorify his name with our wholeness and our gifts. We can move mountains.

LETTER 57

*W*ITHIN YOUR PAIN AND SUFFERING there are many opportunities for healing. It is in your pain that you lose your sense of self and are left with nothing but raw spirit. You, out of habit, curse these darkest days in which you must endure, but I say to you, be of glad heart because you will know a molecular change is coming. You are shaken to the core many times with misery. Hold on with everything you have. The noonday sun is coming and will see you through. There is no law to say you must face these situations in pain. It is okay to be joyous in the discovering that they are necessary phases of life to be dealt with and conquered from a place of peace. Of your human self the trials are too great. This is why you must invite Spirit into your life daily and allow your God to take over. Your human self will falter every time. It is not capable of withstanding such strong emotions that appear in your lives.

Higher and higher our consciences will grow, ultimately reaching that of complete understanding of God and the Christ. Complete oneness with God and each other. Through your efforts know you quicken the processes. It is time . . . and that is why I have come to talk on end about peace, love and forgiveness. The awakening is now. We can dissolve all hate and judgment by working together to remove the dogmas of the past with only one requirement:

To love one another!

Sever from you all those who are unlike love in their words and messages. Cut from you the wagging tongue of intolerance. It has no place in the kingdom. Let the walls of separation, one from another, forever be crumbled into ashes so that my people would serve and worship as one people under God. Let the guilt instilled upon my people be washed away and let them all commune with me personally. It is within each and every child the ability to find that place of quiet solitude where he and his Father in heaven shall communicate and all questions will be answered and not ignored.

Put forth sudden and expectant energy and begin to feel these words reverberate back to you.

I will experience a miracle today

I will open myself up fully to express Spirit today

I will receive a healing today

I will have the opportunity to help one in need today

Put power and expectation into your spoken words and feel the energy within yourself change at a most rapid pace. Believe in the God that loves you and blesses you with all abundance and then thank him for doing so.

LETTER 58

*M*Y MESSAGE TO YOU THIS day and hear me people when I say

YOU ARE THE LIGHT OF THE WORLD

Feel this and know it to be true for you, not your
neighbor, but for you. Close your eyes and feel it . . .
Say it aloud . . . I am the light of the world
I am the light of the world
I am the light of the world

Jesus came and spoke these words, but when he
ascended into the heavens he transferred the power to
you and me through Holy Spirit. You are the light of
the world. Feel the Christ Spirit within you shining so
brightly allowing you to touch every life, every soul that
you come in contact with. Feel the hands of Jesus in your
hands . . . Feel his feet in your feet. See yourself touching
lives with these beautiful hands of Christ light. Allow the
presence of God to work fully through you as you fulfill your destiny of being that light to the world. Accept
your charge and move into the world, spiritually guided.
I illumine your path and ready you a place. Go forth as a
beacon of light to all who are in need. I will never leave
you; draw your strength from me.

LETTER 59

BEGIN TO SEE YOUR BEAUTY reflected back to you. As you are, so shall you see. In your quiet desperation let you always see the light. In a moment's time your whole life can be changed. In an instant . . . transformed. Look for and seek out the glory in the mundane. Lift yourselves to a higher way of looking at things. See with different eyes. Seek the rainbows of life. Your place is beside me. Begin to place yourself there. Act as if you are already beside me so we can work together in unison. Begin to enjoy every moment of everyday. To live with the ultimate desires of your heart and expediently fulfill them with passion. We can achieve this way of being for you, if it is within you to do so. You can stay as you are in a gray existence or you can ask for the life that only God can give, the clarity of purpose that only Spirit can give. Ask and ask and ask until it is done. If you believe that it is possible, never cease asking, beating the floors and crying till there is not one tear left to shed if need be. This is your life you are surrendering and be clear about that. No more holding on and doing it your own way, floundering from place to place. No more shall that way of living be for you. It will be taken from you, forever. You are the light of the world. Blessed are the light workers.

LETTER 60

PRAYER—WHAT IS IT? How DOES it play a significant role in our daily lives? And why should it? To
commune with the Father, to be in that holy presence,
to know beyond a doubt that this is in fact with whom
you speak is beyond words to describe. An experience so
peaceful, so clear, that you would prefer never to come
back from it. How then can an experience like that not
be the most transforming experience your body, mind,
and soul can ever have? These are the reasons prayer is so
important to our human selves. You have to connect with
God and become centered in his love again. As you live
your life out among the world you are led astray naturally
and must reconnect with your God. In this way you stay
steadfast on your own paths to God's glory in your lives.
The more this connection is made the closer to heaven
on earth you become. It is your soul's desire to be in that
presence at all times, never experiencing separation of
any kind from its God. Separation occurs when we are in
judgment, fear, anger or even loneliness, all of which lead
to separate states away from God. You are meant to live
a joyous and complete, harmony-filled life. Prayer is your
key. Some of you will have a negative connotation when I
mention prayer having been brought up in guilt inflicted
religions that judge not only others but themselves as well.
Substitute meditation if it feels better to you. They are
one in the same. Some may speak different words; the

ultimate goal is the same—a greater, more significant relationship with God. Halleluiah.

God waits with open arms to hear from his children who have been lost and led astray. He holds nothing against you, brethren. He only wants to be by your side in every circumstance and every situation. He wants you to hand over your life so that you can begin to live it. Have thankfulness for his love. Oh glory! How our hearts are filled to overflowing.

My message is clear . . . for God so loved us and our world that he came to show us exactly how we could live and that anyone who believes in what he taught and believes that they also can live in oneness with the Father, will never die, but have eternal life. A new life in this new world that will be upon you in the blink of an eye. Let your songs and rejoicing flow from you like fountains. Open yourselves to receiving all of his blessings.

Prayer is the only channel to the Father. It will always be the first step in which Holy Spirit takes over for you, helping and assisting you to communicate with God personally (at a higher level). He has been calling upon you and now is your time to answer. Pray for guidance, pray for one another, pray for gifts of the spirit, and pray for an anointing in your life. Pray with others for peace, clarity, and understanding. A revelation awaits you and the miracles of prayer will come. Imagine yourself on the other side right now and what would you be saying to the Christ if you had the opportunity? What would you talk about? What questions would you ask? Would you thank him for anything or ask that he do something special? This is your beginning prayer. Let it grow from there.

LETTER 61

GLORY, GLORY, GLORY! I SEE angels all around. It is as it was in the day of Joseph, angels manifesting in the skies overhead showing us the way, giving us guidance and assuredness. Sent by God these ethereal beings gently urge us to follow our God-given paths. To reconnect and know that God is an integral part of our lives when we allow him to be. His angels watch expectantly over us, waiting for a time when we need comfort, guidance, or clarity and will believe enough to ask for their help. In conjunction with Holy Spirit they help transform our thoughts, actions and words, but they cannot be effective without our help. They bring to us ideas and messages that we many times discard. Pay attention to the voice within.

LETTER 62

RING ME YOUR CUP AND I will fill it with the treasures of heaven. In this way you will again know
that I am your Lord. What frightens you and keeps you
from your glory? My love penetrates all.

LETTER 63

*D*O NOT KEEP THE GIFTS of the Spirit from my children. It can be their darkest moments, when they completely lose themselves in the anguish, that they are able to receive the gift of Spirit. It can be a time of joy and jubilation that they finally receive clarity. In the stillness I will always come, whether you can acknowledge me or not. The struggle to get to this place with God is the soul's journey and culmination of all experience past and present. A person's path must be ready for this, for when my hand touches you, you are no longer in the dark and have no more excuse to live in spiritual immaturity. You must be prepared to set forth fully, completely, without hesitation on the journey for which you have been chosen, no matter what that looks and feels like. Be patient with yourselves and the process. Come to me in prayer and thanksgiving and we will join together as one when the time is right.

Feed me with the berries of thy knowledge and with the fruit of thy wisdom. Within me is but a woman of simpleness. Grace me with your compassion and understanding. Leave me not to my own devices but give me all that I would ever need from the heavens. Twisted and in confusion are my thoughts that carry me to my next day. Flow through me and cleanse all that is unlike you. Then let me carry the light of the word to nations not known or understood. To glorify only you, dear God, only you. Bring me the peace that will go with me and before me. Let me rise up and perform your good will to the people and not question. Peace go before me and prepareth my way. Take from me my fear and give me the iron will of angels. I shall not sit back and wait while nations and countries devour the earth.

I am the Lord thy God and through faith your light will illumine the world. Peace go with you now.

It is of a time when men cannot lay back on their laurels any longer and let governments and kings decide the fates of nations. It is only one world affected greatly by the individual parts that make the whole. Do you not see how you are connected to this whole and how you can make a difference by having a voice?

Sometimes the smallest things have the greatest impact. Silence is no longer, it is time to speak and be heard. It is time for lands to share resources completely, for the betterment of the entire universe. As children we held on tightly to those things we believed to be rightly ours, but we are no longer children and this is not so any longer. We are one world, one people, and one universe under one God with many names. What belongs to one belongs also to another and so on. This one world consciousness saves lives and resources and brings the peace, love and understanding of one another that you seek. All of mankind wants to be heard and understood. Are you too proud a people to allow that from others unlike you? If a culture does not think as you are they wrong? If they do not look and dress as you, are they ignorant? How much more has your advancement and intellect gotten you? Or has it diminished who you really are? You really have no idea, so I have come to explain and teach you about yourselves. To look at life in a new way, a God-centered way. To look at new perspectives and changed perceptions. This is the way, the truth and the light. Let me lead you to a glorious life on earth. Full manifestation and demonstration in your life now. Process all that I have given you up until this point. Internalize all that I have said and then we will begin again.

PART II

LETTER 64

*L*ET'S TALK ABOUT KAREN'S STORY. Simple life, simple wants and desires. Beaten down by a religion that had no spirit. Broken family, broken marriage, but she had a lot of good times, too. More powerful than all of this was her desire to know God intimately. Not just read about him in books. The quest of 18 years began with a voice . . ."Be as Paul was." That didn't stop her from living the way she wanted, but it made her think there was something there. Years of social climbing, getting married and having a child took center stage for her, but with it came misery. Not a misery of poverty or illness, but the kind most prevalent today. Depression without real cause deeply rooted in the mind. Oh, she thought up every reason possible as to why she was depressed. Her job, her location, her family and on and on it continued. Along the way she and her family tripped in and out of traditional and non-traditional churches causing her awareness to grow with each step. She continued to struggle with joy and happiness in her life and then suddenly the real fun began. An illness of sorts, she was determined not to take pills, wanting to be fully aware of the inner pain and try to figure it all out on a higher level. In frustration she began to pray to me, in helplessness she laid before me. In anger she called upon Holy Spirit to change her at her core and it was done. The voice from her youth reappeared and said, "Go write," and again, "Go write." The third time she listened and my voice began flowing through to her to the pages in front of you. Chosen for her compassion, sense of warmth, and straight talk at times, her love of God, simple values, and willingness to serve.

LETTER 65

*I*N THE DAYS TO FOLLOW it will be as it was in the day of the Lord. A new beginning, a new awakening to one power over all. A power working through man to deliver all of men from the pain and suffering of which they have designed. Follow your hearts and the light that is within them; be pragmatic with your affairs. Reach out to help wherever you are needed. Why can we as a people not see and comprehend? There is so much available to us. The mystics and sages of our time have only begun to touch on the universal treasures. Let us rise up as a people: whole, complete and knowing. Rise up in a constant state of love for one another. Knowing that is our path to freedom and our path home. A softer side of life and living, void of harsh words and actions. Your living should come from the words spoken. Your way made clear by the daily messages sent to you by the God of your understanding. Gravitate towards the voice intended for you, attainable in your time of meditation and prayer.

Do not allow your ideals and opinions to fester within you. You have a feeling of anger towards all that oppose you. This is not your way of right thinking. You must learn to become masters of your human selves. You must master the human desires and come to know yourselves as the Christed children of God. You have wandered so far away from the paths that were intended for you. Remember your relationship to me, how we once were and how we can be again. A race amnesia has occurred and at a great expense to you. Reconnect to your source. Reconnect to me, the bringer of light and all things good in your life. Perish not at the hands of man; rise above where they cannot touch you. Be as my angels and float high above it all.

Heaven is a state of being, a state of mind. Propel yourself to that place and begin learning how to stay there. It will feel strange at first. That is where we dwell, on that higher plane. We welcome you and long for your fellowship with us. I and my Father, and all of the ethereal beings, want for this heaven on earth connection with you.

The more you suppress your worldly, human desires and the more you allow your inner light to focus and guide you, the greater your connection to Source will be. Desire not to be of this world. As I have spoken of this before you will remember. Be in the world, not of it. Desire to please and glorify God. Not for his purpose but for your own. Shake free of the hold you've been brought up in. Seek to have that real relationship with God. Real, true, authentic and personal. Let his Spirit come alive in your life, no longer a dormant entity you have no understanding of. Father God is alive and dwells in all things. Be of my world and not your own.

Pleased am I when even one of you knows and understands what it is I try to teach and one by one it shall be done. Understanding begins as a small drop in the ocean that eventually swells into a wave of knowing.

Listen carefully, children, to what I say. As children of God you bear responsibilities. As you grow in your faith and walk more assuredly on your path you must begin to heed the words that I say. As I give you information you must process and act upon it. There can be no place for uncertainty of purpose. This is why we must perfect our way of communications now. As the days and weeks turn to months and years you will have no doubt which road to travel, which door is right, which path is yours to take. The world would be better served if they were to follow in these footsteps, making prayer a priority, silent contemplation routine, questing after their Christ nature instead of wealth and position. You can prosper in many forms. Do not limit yourself to but one way. Open your heart and mind and take in the fruits of heaven. You prosper even now, though you do nothing to bring it upon yourselves.

LETTER 66

ALTHOUGH THERE ARE MANY PATHS to God they all hinge upon the same foundation of inner truth and love. The inner light expressing through you into form in your physical world, bringing about peace and tranquility in your own life amongst a sea of chaos. This must be accomplished in order to have a relationship of substance. You must have the ability to draw strength from that relationship at a moment's notice for that is how long it takes you to react negatively to circumstances thrown your way. Just a moment and you're off on an earthly tantrum of your own making (hell on earth).

Center yourself first and foremost with God and then your other worldly concerns will melt away. Your life will outwardly reflect what is inwardly important. To be a servant of the whole you need not live in poverty with an attitude of servitude. You only have to know and love the whole in all that you do. In doing that, your life is blessed from all directions. There need not be any false pretenses in loving the whole of God. It will bring you emptiness. Only the sincere will reap the rewards of heaven. Do not predicate your thoughts and actions for the rewards you stand to get. Be true unto yourselves so you can know what that love of God entails. Suffer not at the hand of man. He knows not what is important to a child of God because his priorities are so different he cannot understand. Have a loving heart anyway. Whether they torment or ridicule you, it makes no difference. They are blinded and cannot see. Pray for their clarity. Be not the enemy of man but the peacekeeper, the teacher and the way shower, even as I once was upon the earth. Let the light of love shine brightly before you and let nothing hold you back. Your greatest challenges can be seen within your own heart and mind. This is where your Satan dwells. There will always be confrontation with earthen man, but the greatest confrontations come from within. Let Spirit fight the fight and conquer any wrong thinking you hold on to. Overcome your ways of error and be near me always. In this way we can change all things forever.

Be constant in your love for all people and things; never waiver in your consciousness. Choose the higher and continually grace the world with your higher thoughts, lifting the world consciousness in the process. Not by your own might, but of the might that dwells within you . . . Holy Spirit.

I pray that my people would begin to know the power that has been given to them. The coincidences are nothing short of miracles created by the men who bring them about. You are not as common as you think and your resources are many. Begin to look around and notice the daily miracles that surround you. In doing so you will begin to form miracles of your own. Recognize and appreciate the power than is within you, but also know from whence this power comes. Practice your connection. Practice often throughout your day. Expand your mind and stretch your limitations to the unlimited, for that of good and not evil. Expand your thinking to the ends of the earth and back again. Give credence to your thoughts and ideas no matter how extraordinary. They have validity whether you recognize it or not at this time.

LETTER 67

ANKIND HAS A VERY LIMITED view of his world. When will he learn that it is not limited at all? Things that are right before you have not begun to reach their full potential. Look at the miracles that have been preformed with technology, fiber optics, lasers, plastics, etc. Begin to see the possible in the impossible and the ideas will come. They may sound crazy when they come, but they will come. Let freedom grow by holding nothing back. Your freedom grows as you share all that you have with others. Your communities grow as they share their resources with other communities and so it is with nations. We are one under the same powerful God. By my order I command, ye brethren in Christ, set forth on your mission to bring about peace and oneness in this world. Linger not in your homes of comfort, but set out to teach my words. It is in each person's interest to follow their own path, but collectively join in number to gain strength and courage for which you will all need. My words will not go unheard. My wisdom that I impart upon my people will spread as a wildfire amongst dried trees. Depart now from your wrongdoing and receive my gifts. Do not turn from me, but run towards me never turning back to the life from whence you came. A new life is yours, complete and whole. Re-create, in the Christ way, the life you were meant to lead and joyously embrace it with the passion hidden deep inside you now. Behold you are made anew. Spearhead your campaign to the world now. What is the plan? Let us make it together. From what land to which village in what year shall we follow through. Spreading the love of God is not difficult. Do not fear it for you are never alone when you are filled with the spirit of God. You can afford to take risks when you operate at this higher level.

LETTER 68

*And the love of God was upon me in an instant
just by changing my focus to him.*

MY ONE CONCERN OF TODAY is the way in which you are living. Live fully, expressing completely. You are holding back all that is within you. Follow every instinct for just one day and see what will happen. Have no fear of talking to people. Say hello and look them in the eyes. Have no fear because I am with you. Send love to everyone—send it from your heart. Take no offense if you think they don't receive it. They will in due time.

LETTER 69

*T*ODAY I WAS TAKEN TO a most magnificent hall in heaven reaching high with stained glass windows of gold. There was intricate detail everywhere with no sign of concrete. This hall was long and filled with light. Wise men and angels lined along each side and in the center of the room was a fontanel. I was seated in a beautifully carved chair of dark wood when the Christ came and led me to the center of this great hall with everyone watching. He placed upon my forehead, in the sign of the cross, the heavenly water from the fount. The Christ spoke and said, "In the name of the Father, the Son, and the Holy ghost, I baptize you as I also baptized John." So filled with love and emotion, I cried emotionally.

I realized in a moment that all those present were actively involved in helping our transitions here on earth, they were the ones speaking through me and I thanked them for that. I heard one of them say, "The angels rejoice for your sacrifice of self this day." I thought this strange because it hasn't felt like a sacrifice. I thought they might know something about my future that I did not know (besides everything that is).

Then the Christ said, "I baptized you in the name of the Father, the Son and the Holy Ghost because you will take my message to the world. You asked for your Christ nature to shine forth and I have created that more evidently in you through this baptism."

LETTER 70

You are a gift to the world
Somewhere between night and day
In the shadows lay . . . a soul

SOMEWHERE BETWEEN DARKNESS AND LIGHT, hiding, there are souls waiting to be found, thirsting for light. Find them and bring them to me that they may live eternally also.

LETTER 71

*L*EAD THEM TO MY WORD; an utterance of truth to be given them, my children. Spirit leads the way and will manifest before you a great and divine calling. Allowing life to propel forward. Have patience for these things to pass. Guard your temples well, dear brethren, for they will be subject to much discord and anger. Stand firmly on holy ground where the torment cannot touch you. Fear of all things should be admonished. Rise higher in your attitudes and reactions to life. Create a solitude around you that travels wherever you go. Focus on God to bring this about for your selves. Drink in the living waters that surround you, not only to quench an insatiable thirst, but also to cleanse your temple from all that is not right.

Build not a fortress around yourselves for it not only keeps others out, but will also keep you locked within. This is not the fulfilling life that was given you. In order for you to live fully you must open the doors wide to your heart, not only to the heavens, but also to one another. It is of course the wish of every angel to give and receive love from you, but it is even greater to give and receive that same love to each other. It is easy to love God, the giver of light and all things good. How then does it look from heaven when you open your hearts to love your neighbor? Favor no one and love all.

Significance is only temporary while your focus shifts from one to another; one thing, one person, one treasure. Our hope is that all things become significant to you because all things are God given; that creating signifi-cance in all things would transcend who you are to a new extraordinary level of consciousness.

Gather in groups to acknowledge one another's uniqueness, to support one another's walk with God and bring down from heaven the instruction most needed to follow in the footsteps of truth.

You were not placed on this earth alone. Had that been best I would have made it so. You were placed in the company of beautiful people and spirits, just like you. This was not intended to teach you seclusion and isola-tion, but co-habitation and co-creation with one another and with God. Unity, love and sharing in all things. Com-munity, higher visions for a higher existence on earth. Environmental collaboration on plans that don't exhaust or diminish natural resources. Preservation of beauty and land because you know these places facilitate peace and God's presence to all people.

Live here, with me, in the ethers and welcome all who would come as a brother in Christ. Dream of this perfect and possible world that one civilization can create because they found God in their hearts and decided to share it among all men. One civilization praising one God, cry-ing halleluiah and singing, "Holy is our Father in heaven." Praising him for the restoration of their souls. Amen

LETTER 72

*A*S JESUS AND SOME OF his followers were making a trip across barren land a sand storm came upon them making it difficult to proceed. Jesus stopped saying, "Let us wait out this storm and go forth when it has settled." Some of the followers reminded him that there awaited a great crowd in the town they were to visit that evening and that they would be late if they did not continue. Jesus spoke again saying, "The word and deeds of God transcends all, even the minds of waiting men. My Father goes before me to prepare these people you speak of and even though they be weary of waiting they will stay and those who leave will return being glad that they did so."

The group traveling with Jesus sheltered themselves for only a little while as the storm passed and they were able to journey onward. The skies did darken before they reached their destination and the followers were amazed as the crowd was even larger than they had anticipated. The people were filled with joy when they saw that Jesus had arrived. Every spot of ground was taken up and up front were the sick and dying. Jesus sat with them and spoke to them in a soothing voice, touching their hands and feet, their heads and bodies, casting out all illness and disease among them. The presence of the Father, the Son and the Holy Spirit was great within this place and all were blessed with a measure of Spirit, as it was strong and overflowing. Jesus stood and began praying over the multitude, prayers of thanksgiving to the Father. "Let not one man leave this place without your full measure of love and grace having touched their lives, Father. For you are merciful . . . the love and light of the world. Let us give you all the glory and not lose sight of the blessings and abundance you provide us in all things."

Jesus wept with emotion and overcome with love for his people. He fell to his knees continuing to pray and praise God. All that were there were filled to overflowing with the Spirit of God and could not be rid of it had they wanted to. Miracle upon miracle took place that evening and for weeks and months thereafter.

All were exhausted and weary as they made camp that night outside the city. Visitors came to see Jesus all throughout the night as he was unlike any other they had ever seen and wanted more of what he had to offer. "I instruct you now to go and speak to your God in heaven and receive all that you need from him. I am but the teacher and the way shower. I am not needed for you to receive your infilling of spirit, life and love. All comes from the Father. Partake in all that is available to you and have faith that it comes to you now. Peace be with you on your journeys home."

> All among them were pleased and slept few
> hours before journeying home the next day.
> Find your way amongst thorn bushes and
> flowers
> Preparing for the un-preparable
> Expect to live long and happy
> Filling your baskets with bread let love always
> guide your way
> Feel peace at each moment and be patient
> with your growth

Gaze upon your immortality often
Be a leader among men and suffer for cause
Because you love

In your life there will be those days in which you feel hopeless. Reign in your emotions and tighten your lip. Your hidden strengths remain untapped and underdeveloped. Begin by seeing yourself raised up from the mire, a glorious light being, floating above the earth. As you look down upon your life you see that many things you deemed important are not necessarily so from this perspective. When in difficulty always lift yourself higher and gain a new perspective. Joy awaits you there.

LETTER 73

*W*HEN THE TIME OF YOUR awakening comes, you will be surrounded by great color. Spectrums of light from all around you. Things that had no light will shine brightly and you will be amazed.

Your faith is small and you do not believe what I am saying as true. Your mind is always flooding your thoughts with doubt. I shall go away from you and come back when you are ready. In these days, your human body is so dead to my presence. So desensitized to me that you cannot feel my touch upon you. Must we always go through this ritual before you believe it is I that speaks to you? Lose your doubt and know in your inner most knowing that even though there is no way of knowing all that I tell you it is still from God and no other. As you continue all things will become clear.

The disappointments that I feel are not from you but from the powerlessness of my people. Caught alone with all the forces of mankind preying upon them, they cannot find their way and this I never imagined would be. I sent my Son to show you the way. I have sent divine messages throughout the ages. Man has not been heeding my words and is lost in darkness. Those who see the light have a responsibility out of love for one another, to show mankind the way to freedom and complete happiness. Divine guidance in their lives leading to their divine purposes. Respect yourselves enough to allow yourselves to flourish in the lives that you long for. Discover all of those things your soul longs to do.

LETTER 74

A VOLATILE TIME IS COMING. A test of wills, a test of faith. Not by God, but of your own leadership. You will know who your allies are and who are not. A cumulative shakedown of sorts in which relations that have been formed will either withstand the pressure of crumble beneath the weight.

Have faith that God will meet you and all your loved ones as you pass to the other side. There will be much sorrow, but your grief will transform the lives of every generation to follow.

Before the temple of the Almighty you will be brought before and the light will shine so brightly as to blind the eyes of earthly men, but you will gaze upon the presence of the Lord in spirit form and all understanding will be transferred and given to you all in that instant. You will immediately long to help others you have left behind and will send messages of hope and answers to their questions. You will experience complete love for all things and take your place among the angels to assist the heavens in any way possible. Your soul never dies and longs to help you transform matter turning hate to love, anger to peace, all things transformed for good. That is why your soul came upon earth, to help. Do not disappoint it. Do those things your soul has called you to do. Do not lose this opportunity to make a difference, lest you stand before the bright light of God's altar and be disappointed in yourselves.

God energy is pure love, and as you stand amidst this love you will know in an instant what you have left undone. You will know if you lived your life to the fullest and after judging yourselves you will run as quickly as possible to help those left behind on earth so that they may live their lives to the fullest. This is love.

But I say love now! Don't hesitate. Be a part of life now, not an after-product of what life has dealt you. Be the dealer, the captain with the courage to listen to God instead of man. Turn from the popular opinions of man, the opinions of God are timeless and do not change. They have no fear of current events or worldly concerns. Only that of a higher place and time. Be concerned only with those things of right and good and God. Be forever blessed for it and know that the indwelling Christ is within you. Place in my heart your love and forgiveness of one another, place in my hands your fears.

I want to speak now of the life of Jesus.

In Galilee there was a festival with great dancing and festivities. The dancers wore elaborate costumes, including headdress. Jesus was amongst those present and enjoyed immensely seeing everyone have such a good time. He smiled and laughed and communed with friends, family and children throughout the day, enjoying every moment of the celebration. By evening most were tired, but Jesus had an untiring energy. Many had returned to their homes when a caravan of men looking as though they were passing through town approached Jesus. They approached the campfire where Jesus sat and knew in a moment who he was. They had heard stories throughout the kingdom of this man from Galilee. They had many questions as well as accusations. They felt as a devout Jew, he was breaking many Jewish traditions and for such a proposed Holy Man having too much fun. As they jested and continued with their mockery, Jesus never lost sight of his love for them and it was visible to the men around him that they offended him not, but that Jesus recognized them as ignorant to the ways of God and that they had no understanding or basis from which to understand. Jesus politely and quietly answered each question and then rising up began to touch each and everyone present at his fire saying, "You are the children of the living God. Blessed are you who believe in my Father and from henceforth take no ill will out into the world. It is by no accident that you have found me this day in the city of Galilee. Go, my brethren, and sin no more."

Jesus spoke these words to many men whom he had helped to transform. The words contained no magic in them, but nonetheless produced magical results to the people in luck enough to hear them. Traveling throughout the land Jesus always had the opportunity to heal, but preferred teaching so that all men might heal the sick and not depend completely upon him. He never longed to be the object of worship for the miracles he preformed, but only to glorify God, the Father of all. To show and demonstrate the power available to all of us when we tap into the God center of ourselves. Even the resurrection, the ascension into heaven, is possible to those who attain the Christ nature. Jesus came to show us how. Let us begin to study the ancient texts. Those manuscripts that were hidden and put aside years ago will reappear and be made available so that all might know information from the mystic ages. Lost to those who would control all power; their lives already damned for doing so. A great re-awakening on a global scale will occur when these ancient texts are released and others found. I will lead scientist on the path of rediscovery, the greatest scientific exploration of mankind, for they will be found.

I asked if I could not interpret some of those ancient records now and I got:

If all things are energy, and they are, molecules are just molecules interacting in relation to one another at different levels and speeds. Become one with all and your molecules change to become and create that one thing. Create a higher dimension that you can levitate to, thus creating space below you. The masters studied and perfected this for hundreds of years proving its possibilities yet they are not widely recognized for their spiritual mastery and teachings.

Transporting of one's physical body to another place takes a great skill and mastery of your cells and molecular make up. Once again creating a space in which your body can travel to through a higher dimension of time and space. Re-align your molecules to this higher frequency so that travel is possible. Your form will not leave its current position but will enter into a state of shutdown thus looking as though you are sleeping. You can either come back if you choose or decide to stay where you have traveled. It is similar to telepathy. Even now you are capable of sending thoughts (which is energy and so it your body). Once perfected begin to send your images. A person need not know how to receive these images, they will just appear

LETTER 75

*D*EATH MEANS LITTLE TO ME as it does to you. Centuries have been defined by it. Dates of importance memorialize it. It is no different from a common ailment. No more or no less significant. It is good that these layers upon which you wear cease at some point. You do not realize how daunting they are. Be happy for those who have gone on before you. They lead exemplified lives and are full of happiness. Let them pass with your blessings and let their passing be a blessing unto you. It is an opening of a new door for both of you. The void is excruciating at times because your love for them is so great. I do not patronize you when I say find God and ask him fill the void in your heart. To comfort you and hold you when the pain is too great to bear. This is not the end, but the beginning. Allow yourself to see it and it will be so.

Laughter over the small things your loved ones did will bring them closer to you in the world. Laughter transcends time and space for the moment and brings all in alignment. Laugh more often and more fully. Bring joy to yourself and those around you.

View death as the renewing process it was meant to be to your soul. The gathering up of the light it has lost and misplaced over its years upon the earth. Rejoice and make celebration a part of your ritual, a celebration of having known them as they lived, and a celebration that they now get to go home and be in God's presence.

The time is now that we put away the old ways and incorporate the new. Nothing has changed except the perceptions. Change now and save yourselves from self-inflicted torment.

LETTER 76

*S*TILL IN THIS DAY THERE is no way of knowing everything there is to know, so limited in our beliefs and so ineffective because of it. So involved with the day-to-day struggles of life we give little thought or attention to the greater scheme. Our focus should always be on the greater things of life and never on the things that continue to rob us of it. Connect to every situation through the higher avenue. Be the observer. In that way you can truly access and understand the situation.

Example–if you have a difficult work life and you relate to it on a very human level, all you see as a result is a very irritating, energy draining experience. However, if you relate to work through your higher self you see a peaceful experience where your expertise is needed to fulfill the needs of others. In this state, you have a hard time seeing what all the stress is about.

Is this not a form of mastery over your own environment? It is not denial in any way because you are not ignoring your duties, but simply approaching them from a much higher level. As you connect with Source, and know it as your source and not your job, you consciously decide to work for a higher energy throughout your day. " I happen to be at a job that pays me to work for my higher good," you will say. "It is but one avenue of my prosperity."

Fear nothing will take your prosperity away. It is far

more than a state of mind. It is real. I have blessed many of my followers with riches upon earth; my kings, my leaders, and many of my teachers. There are many who do not desire such treasures on earth; it is enough whatever they have. Don't feel guilty if you have great wealth, only share in great measure with the ones who have less. Many of you have great gifts and are paid well for your talents. It pleases me to see you prosper. Live a God-filled life, love all people, even those less fortunate. Choose for yourself which life you will lead and be happy with it. The power has been given unto you to choose wisely for who it is that you are. Be comfortable with the choice, knowing it was you who made it. Now having set your sites come higher to connect with the heavens and make it so. Stake claim to all that I would have you inherit. Make it so in heaven and it will be so on earth.

Each person has a persona they project out into the world. Every one of them different. Look for your God-given persona. What does that look like? Does your prosperity have anything to do with that? Yes or No. Either could be right, depending on who you are inside. I only want you to look and know. To do this takes time; give it to yourself as a gift.

Since the coming ages are to be a rebirth and re-awakening of an entire subculture of the universe, it can only stand to reason that there must be a re-awakening and rebirth of your souls to a higher ground. Not all will land there, but through this process many will.

Seek and pray to know that higher part of who you are and get to know it more intimately. Almost as if one side is dark and one side is light, long to see the light more evidently in your life so that you may learn to live only in the light, doing away with the dark altogether.

In our haste we lose center, pulled off course with the slightest wind. By dedicating your life to loving God you choose not to falter when the storms come. Acceptance of the Christ spirit that you are, with no doubt and no question, brings complete joy into your life. Do you not want that for yourselves? Is it not good enough for who you are? Come to me and be my companion now and forever.

LETTER 77

Live not in fear of a punishing God, but of one whose love cannot be described in earthly words. Only the angels can speak of his beauty and have words to describe it. I live with a knowing in my heart that I am taken care of you no matter what my outward circumstances might be. I live as a soldier in an army, asking no questions because I believe they will be answered in due time. I live because I've been shown a love like no other, an overwhelming presence in my mind and in my body that will not be ignored nor shall I ever want for that. I am a part of the heavens and they me, allowing for the integration of both worlds on earth. The precious time I spend in both worlds creates a cover of wisdom around me. I live in this shroud of insight from God, extremely careful that I do not lose sight of my Father in Heaven who leads me.

Falter not in your belief that I am who I say I am. Jehovah, Emmanuel, the Christ. Blessed will your days be, those who believe.

Now go and lead your own people by faith because of the love shown to you. Not by fear and thoughts of suffering. Search the beauty in God's presence. Seek out his holiness amongst you. See how his hand touches the waters at sunset. Witness his immense stature as you gaze upon mountains. Feel the swell of his heart as you watch the oceans roll. Even nature caresses your skin with the wind out of love for you. Will you return your love to him in this gentle way?

He longs to feel your touch, to know your acknowledgement of him in your life. To show gratitude when things are going well and when things are upside down. His love never changes least of all with your circumstances.

Be open to new avenues in which you can receive blessings. Be aware of them around you. In prayer ask to be shown all of these things important to you. Ask to be given answers to every question. This is important for you to do on many levels. Listen for your answers no matter how odd they seem, take appropriate action. Take time to pray, take time to relax the body, letting it float upward towards heaven. You may not feel, see, hear, or experience anything on the conscious level however, things are happening each and every time you take a moment to reconnect with God. It cannot help but be so, even if you do not notice it. Be of glad heart in your prayers with sincere thanksgiving. Let that feeling of thankfulness flow throughout your body giving you joy. I know many of you cannot bring together enough strength to utter the words "Thank you God," but say it anyway. Say it over and over again and you will feel the strength of the heavens coming to you. Believe in the power of the spoken word and claim for yourself words worth speaking and thus a life worth living. Diligently choose every word you utter. Your reality, whether real or imagined, matters not. It begins with you and your thoughts. Let your thoughts be your constant prayer. Why must you leave my presence? Over time and with practice you will never have to leave unless you choose to.

Let go of who you think you are, let go of all your preconceived notions about what your life will be like. If you want a joyous, God-filled life, truly without reservation, go back to the simplest yet hardest law of all.

Put God first in your life above all people and things. Like Abraham who was willing to sacrifice his son in order to completely follow his inner guidance, you too are asked to go through life having that sort of faith in God. When we hear clearly God's will we are not to sit back and wait, but move forth swiftly with intention and blessing. Heed the gentle prod of God's hands pushing you ever so slightly into his direction. His direction will always lead to the softer more secure side of your life. Follow without hesitation. Love knowing from whence your guidance comes and be assured it is from God, but also make sure your heart is in the right place. Discover with me our sacred place. To be together in conversations that can last for as long as you like. Bring all of your worries and lay them before my table. We shall discuss every detail—good and bad. We will solve every problem and bring about forgiveness for every long forgotten ill. We will heal you and bring you your calm. We will show you a life of possibilities strange in some ways, glorious in others. Bring your palette on which to display the many hues and colors we will show you. You will not want to forget one detail. Let us find our sacred place and receive our comfort there all the days of our life.

LETTER 78

BE AT PEACE, YOUNG SAVIORS, be at peace. Your journey is not as foreboding as you envision. You lack the clarity to see all that will transpire. Lackluster is the word that comes to mind. Sharpen your skills and focus on your individual abilities to rise to a new level in which you will see and feel and hear clearer than ever before the words of heaven. You will grasp true meaning without hesitation. Seek my presence often that I may teach you all you will ever want to know.

My young children, drift to me in your dreams at night and let me tell you the stories of life eternal. The sweetest peace your soul will ever know. Take comfort and rejuvenate completely for the day comes and takes you from me. The obstacles of living you must overcome, but not alone. I am there with you, lifting your feet, moving you from side to side that you may avoid the pitfalls. And when you collapse in my arms once more and sleep brings you comfort and resolve, I am there . . . touching your creviced brow, loving you into wholeness, giving you all that you need so that you may once again face the day and all that it brings with the strength and assuredness that your God is with you, and even as you sleep, goes before you.

Letter 79

Brick four sides strong will surround what is left of my living word. Brethren upon brethren will know when Christ comes again. My words will be found and sacred they will be. The lands on all sides will shrink back as man realizes their mistakes. Clarity will be yours, young saviors. Expect it and treat it well for these are the gifts of the Lord. Give thanksgiving and praise and lead your people out of Canna. The words will profess The One true God of all and every head will bow in reverence to it.

For now be earnest in keeping peace, helping others and giving love. The angels and I will be walking amongst you, leading and guiding your way. You will not know it is I, but consciousness will prod you into knowing at a later time that you have encountered a heavenly being sent by God to rescue, guide and love you. It is of no consequence that you know who we are now. In due time we well reveal ourselves to you.

Be pragmatic in these situations. Your utmost sincerity, faith and trust are needed to see us through.

LETTER 80

*I*T WAS IN THE BEGINNING that I gave you all under-standing, but you could not hold and sustain that level for long because of your ego and your humanness. In fleeting moments you remember your knowledge and begin to recall your true essence . . .

LETTER 81

FEAR NOT THE TURMOIL WITHIN your own heart; it is I the Father who brings you home. Your path is clear and lies before you. Uncover the earth that has lain upon your path with its influences. The light of heaven illumines it when you ask for it to be done. Flip the switch, connect the wires and be on your way.

I have given you thoughts and ideas of which you have made no use. Your genius is not yet utilized because you fear failure and know not that these ideas come from me. I do not wish for your failure but success in all things in which you endeavor. You have no vision of how your needs will be met, but I say unto you, worry not, I have only the best in mind for you. I will show you where to receive your daily sustenance and I will show you how your next ideas will be fulfilled. Trust in me and none other so that I may show you your vision. Even with best intentions others attempt to guide and help you, but it is only I, and the Father, that can teach you truth enough to lead and guide you. Discover my ways for yourself so that you might live fully, feeling my complete presence in you daily, showing, guiding, prodding, teaching you the truth about you.

Your importance upon the earth, there are no words to convey. Each of you has a divine idea within you that has to be unleashed, learned, and acted upon or you will always have a feeing of emptiness and failure, no matter how much you achieve on the worldly plane. Strip thyself of all falseness and false Gods that hinder and hold you. You have greatness upon the earth. I have told you since the beginning of time that your greatness comes from heaven and your rewards reside there too. It is not impossible to have these things upon the earth, but it is impossible as long as you worship and long for the things of earth over those things in heaven. Your life is but an avenue for choices each day. Your power to direct your own lives is unimaginable to you, but know that at any moment you have the abilities to change everything about you. Come to me and ask what those changes should be and trust that I lead you in the direction of your good. A beautiful new life awaits you when you lift higher and ask God which direction you should take, which decision to make. Live your life in joyous expectation of the next miracle in your life.

Believe that there can be magic in your life; a magical experience of living in the light. The Christ came to prove to us that such a life could truly be. Satisfy your soul's longing to have that relationship with God that the Christ demonstrated and said we could have also.

LETTER 82

BEAUTY IS BUT ONE WAY in which to measure your own fulfillment. It is there as a guide that you might recognize the space in which you live. That arena in which you have chosen to act out your life. The more beauty you can see and recognize, the more connected you are to your source thus experiencing fulfillment in your life. The ability to see beauty in the mundane or simple tasks of living is a gift you are able to give yourself as you follow your path in God. Being true to yourself is but one step. Acknowledging your own beauty is another and seemingly much more difficult. Upon your face see your soul smiling and within your eyes see the sparkle of God within.

Lose not hope if you stray from your path. Walk with the knowledge that every footstep has been prepared for you. Your beauty is awe inspiring when you believe this and let it shine. Then all things become as beautiful as you desire them to be. Your heaven exists in your state of mind, which brings forth your many blessings from heaven. Naturally you must learn to recognize and acknowledge those blessings as well. Many slide through life in a state of happenstance. This should not be the state for a child of God. We have the ability to change all things in our life; nothing is by chance. Choose to change it in accordance with what is right and good for you and you will know and experience a love and freedom like you have never known. The understanding will astound you, the blessings amaze you. Lay down your ideas, your will, and your life and go forward with the life intended for you. See beauty in all things knowing that it is God that makes it evident to you.

The Breath knows long before you which direction you will choose, but allows you to change your direction at any time. Do not think all is decided, it is not and you have choices, however, Holy Breath knows of all of them and if asked will help you find the one of right. No one wishes to flounder and make mistakes. They only want to fly freely on wings of angels and succeed in all they do. Find the higher road and follow it without fail. The road to the higher is available to you now. Be resourceful and let no man steer you from it. Be strong when tempted; you are no longer the lesser man, but Spirit filled. You have no need for the desires of the flesh. Lift beyond them. Thank the heavens that this is so and that you have no desire to squander after the worldly life, but live to satisfy your spirit and soul. Be pleased with yourselves and your progress and continue to diligently search for the deeper meaning. I will always be there waiting to show you.

LETTER 83

FEEL THE HURTS OF THE world and have compassion for them. The world must experience their hurt for a time before letting go of those feelings. Judge them not as weak, but on their journey to their own discoveries. I have shown all of man an easier way of living that does not need to be that of suffering but that of joy. Be cognizant of your surroundings. Be aware of the time and space you allow people and things of lower energies to take from you. Shelter your soul from negative influences and thought processes. Give value to your life and begin eliminating all destructive behaviors, mindsets, and people of lesser vibrations (this does not imply any one is lesser, but the lower energies will drain you). Safeguard all that is true and valuable, your mental attitudes, your energy, your ability to see and feel clearly. These can be damaged if not kept safe.

I do not say to become a recluse in search of serenity and safety, but become more powerful in the ways of God that you might easily repel all that is not of God. Your patience and your faithfulness will prove very valuable to you in days to come. Sending a message of love to those around you, bring them peace and a longing for home. You do not see it as yet because it is not time. All that Christ came to show you was love, patience and faithfulness in God, the Father, because he cared and wanted us to have life more abundantly.

LETTER 84

*N*OW IS A TIME OF jubilation. A time for thanksgiving and recognition of the many blessings which come.

Keep favor amongst you for it is in the interest of all. Your selfishness does not bode well with the harmony of the planet, but creates discord and disharmony. Take a moment to reflect on your own actions with regard to selfishness. You are a holy instrument of God yet you stand in your own way. Step aside, time and again and lose your selfish pride and egotism so that I may work the miracles of which I've come to work through you. I have not seen your commitment to me of late. Schedule life around your commitment to me and be blessed for it. If your day is to start an hour later or an hour earlier, let it be so. You are anxious and nervous about life and work and the day in front of you and you will know immediately it is because you are living without me and your focus is not on God, but on your own faculties again. You have already discovered how weak and non-productive that is. It is just as it was in the days of old when I was upon the earth. It mattered not how I taught or what I was able to perform, your humanness could not comprehend so it could not hold on to the truth that would set men free. Man has changed yet he changes not. Live for understanding of my truth. Seek to understand the higher meaning of what I came to say and teach. I will light up the night with the knowledge of my words so that they can be made clearer to the masses. They are made ready to hear the yin and the yang of my words. The obvious meaning along with the underlying meaning and they will recognize that it is I that speak a truth no different from before, but more complete. Encompassing their hearts.

Be proud of the spirit that lies upon you. Do not hide it from the world that needs it now. Be bold in your deliverance and mighty will the hand of God be upon you and create in you a maker of true men. Be obedient in my word and it will not be taken from you. Glory unto the king of kings. Tarry not but go, sayeth the Lord, visiting each church and denomination sharing my love of all and new promises of truth.

This will cause much pain as well as joy for you. People will scold and harass you with hatred and ill will, like you have not seen before in your life. Others will love and support you. Come to me for your every need and comfort and I will give it to you, seeing that you receive all good things in light of your sacrifices. If only one man comes to know God and have a personal relationship with him, you have done right by the heavens and your heart.

LETTER 85

AND THE ANGEL OF THE lord came upon her, a woman of years and spoke saying, "All that the Father has given unto you shall skip a generation and be given to your grandson, a blessing of the lord upon him." She was wise as this gift of sight had been given her from God and the angel did say, "Teach him all that you were taught by the Holy Spirit. Allow him to falter for he will always return to that which feeds him the wisdom of God."

What will become of my son that he would receive nothing from me? And the angel spoke, "Be of glad heart as your own son will be for he will know this comes from God and no other. Fortunate his son will be and he will be glad for it."

The angel left and time passed as the young grandson grew and was thirsty for knowledge of all things and the old woman taught him all that she knew. As he grew in stature and in knowledge his faith in the lord grew strong also. His understanding of all things was mighty and he began to teach and prophesy to the people.

He took a wife who boar him sons and he was blessed by the lord. His vision was strong and made known to the people all that God would have them know for their own safety and knowledge. The man's demeanor was that of God's as he did commune with God daily. As his life was turned for worse many times he did not stumble, but held steadfast in his great knowledge and understanding of the things of life. He glorified God and lived as he was told. His gifts and obedience brought hope to a people with none and a love of God that was shared.

Be steadfast in your faith, young children; learn to listen to my words for your life, daily. Your ability to bring hope and love to the people has been given to you as a gift from heaven. Know that it is there within you to be given. Be aware of your own visions and ask for their clarity that you may show the people what I have said. Everyday you learn more about life and living it. Share with the world what you learn.

Bring me the voice of indifference and I shall shatter it into a million pieces of compassion. I can lead you through the hard times when no one wants to hear. It is only because it is much easier to deny the need for change in their lives than it is to change. Higher seekers look to change it, but most do not seek it, but need it just the same.

LETTER 86

*W*HAT IS RIGHT FOR US is right for God. You do not have to be concerned if it is right in the eyes of others. We need only do and speak what is right for us. If you do that which is right with God, it will always be right for you.

Where does our focus lie? With what others will think or say if we do the will of God. How embarrassed we should be as a human race to think that way. When did we lose complete sight of the meaning of our lives? It has never been to please man; it has never been to be exalted on earth with titles and position. Only in doing the will of the One do we serve ourselves truthfully.

"But we cannot hear the voice of God," the people say. "How are we to follow it?"

We run daily in chaos when all we need to do is stop, and listen. God wants to talk to us. God wants us to be able to hear his voice, but he will not keep chasing us. We must stop to hear first.

Usually something drastic happens in our lives to make us slow down and take a moment to get closer to him. To hear his instruction for our lives. If you cannot hear God, listen again. If you still cannot hear him, listen again and again and again.

I thought God couldn't get through because of my own voice I heard in my mind. I didn't know God WAS that voice in my mind. Not the itinerary keeper that is in there saying you have to go to the post office, grocery store and oh, don't forget the dry-cleaning. God's voice is gentle and loving and when you ask a question he has the answer. His voice is the voice of reason and comfort.

Listen again, ask a question, write the question down, and then listen for the answer. Our lives are more than what we know them to be. Our relationship with God is more than we are experiencing today.

"People" talk of being saved or born again. Is it out of fear? Fear of going to a fiery place? Or is it fear of disappointment to their families? There are many good people that have been born again out of fear and God wants you to know that fear has nothing to do with it. The glorious relationship that he wants to have with you is about living with his presence deep inside your heart day after day, for the rest of your earthbound life; asking, seeking, studying for your peace and understanding of life and discovering how God wants you to live it. In living God's way, you are living it at the highest level possible for you. There is no other way for you to live happily, joyfully, and contented.

LETTER 87

I WILL FLOW THROUGH THE LAND like a mighty river and into your hearts my love will grow to overflowing. I can save you from the storm should you have faith enough and trust me. Our time is important to the outcome of who you are to become. Fragile and faint hearted are you as you hurt and become more confused at life. Lying on the ground your lifeless body is waiting to be picked up. Listen to my call; ask me to pick you up and with the power of angels by your side it will be done. Offer unto me all your grievances of others as well as yourself and I will forgive them all.

You do not know who I am. You do not know until it is revealed to you. In your prayers ask that I be shown to you in completeness and be prepared to be knocked down once more by the Holy Ghost that will sweep through you and around you. But when you arise, you will never be the same. For the glory of the Lord in me shall now be in you, forever.

Take the cup which I offer you now, the cup of righteousness, the cup of life everlasting. Place me at the forefront of your lives, dear ones. Let me be first to guide you.

LETTER 88

*I*N AND WITH THE SPIRIT of God my words are made manifest through you, the people of my Father. Hearken your hearts to his presence among you now. Feel the energies changing around you. See the consciousness of the world raising. No longer are you hunters and scavengers, but a people of peace and love for one another. Can you not accept that this is who you are? There need not be more to who you are. God is lifting you up each time you recognize this in yourselves. When you reach out, when you seek no recognition for your good deeds, when you love just for the sake of loving and not for what you will receive in return, the Father lifts you up. I see the shift all around. I feel the love. Let us rejoice and give thanks that your day upon the earth is coming.

We know not the hour, but you have made it clear how. I have been overcome with the feeling of complete joy as you show me the moment of realization in my heart. The moment I know and recognize what is happening—the ascension of all Christed souls; all of those believing in you, all of those children who love you inherently without ever seeing you. The joy floods my eyes with tears.

LETTER 89

HE LORD IS NEVER WANT for words to say, only souls to listen. Oh, that all that hear could multiply their ears by one thousand so that the word would spread to all. Any other Gods that you hold dear in your life need to be gone from you. There is no time to be led away by such things. I do not speak of golden statues of the past, but the golden statues of today. Do not be seduced by your homes and worldly things such as others around you hold dear. Release yourselves from the hold they still have over you. God does not say to sell all that you have and live the life of a pauper. He says get your priorities straight, dear ones. What takes you away from your families and your time with God? A job or two that pays for the things "you think" you need and deserve? The things that are standard for a man of your stature? Release yourself from that way of thinking and let God reward you according to your character, not according to men of the world. Make your supposed priorities a priority in life and stop deceiving yourselves. Make no excuses and stop telling yourselves lies as to why God and family are not first on the list. In truth they are much lower on your list of priorities.

The world needs you now. They need to see that part of you, unguarded, that is so beautiful and angelic, full of joy and giving.

Be determined in matters of the soul. Seek excellency in yourself in that area as much as you do your vocation. Be relentless that you might receive a raise in consciousness as you seek a raise at work. If you are diligent, the raise in consciousness is guaranteed.

Be selective in your daily lives about all things. Be conscious . . . of all things. Live in a state of awareness. Know the choices you are making at a conscious level. Monitor your thoughts, your friends, the food you eat, the company you work for and their ethics. Re-evaluate the way you speak, think, converse etc.

Cleanse the house of God for I dwell therein with you. It gives me pain to receive your painful emotions. Give calm and solace where there is none. Be with me so that you would make better choices for your life. Anticipate a change for good in doing so.

I saw a land in which there were equal parcels divided. Every man and every Son of every family had their own equal share to tend. It looked to be about 10 acres each. When I asked what this was I was seeing I was told it was a land that would come to be. Each man would have an equal amount of the worldwide pie, so to speak. Global sharing will occur in a day to come. We need more love of one another, we need more giving, and the world needs to become even smaller to us. What affects one area will affect another.

Will it be equal parts of land? I don't know. It may be equal land, equal houses, and equal bank accounts. There was a strong feeling that money will not even be involved. We may possibly realize that what I do for you does not directly correlate to you paying me. I would get my abundance from above or from things other people would do for me. I don't know how it would work exactly, but I can't wait to see.

LETTER 90

THE LIFE AND THE LOVE of God reign down victorious upon his people. Depart from your ways and follow mine. Oh, Israel, I have prepared your place amongst the clouds. You have long been away from me. The human desire so strong that thou didst not hear my calling for you. It is here and now that I call to you. Infiltrate to the lands I have given to you. The Holy Ghost will go forth and keep you. Surround thyself with holy cloth and wine. Feel my presence abiding with you always. My Son and I love the people of Israel with all our hearts and find peace in knowing you are going home. Finish your business. Prepare for your journeys now. Begin and then wait for the cause of which you will bear witness to. Your neighbor may think you crazy; prepare anyway.

Stock thy cupboards as well as thy purse and make no miscalculation, for you will be a people of persecution. A target for hate. Stand strong with one another, as you have done so in the past. You will need your strong faith in the years to come.

I do not wish for your suffering, but for the peace and the promise of an abundant, joyous life. Your Father of fathers will light the flame over you once again and you will instantly know that I am with you. The world will know that I am with you.

Feast upon my blessings in this world and take with you what ere you need, being an honest and faithful people. Lend whatever you can to your neighbor in need. It is your way of sharing my blessings.

I am a vessel sent to you to provide all that you need in days to come. A vessel of wisdom and truth with the intent to yield warning to you. Take hold!

I have so much to give to you. I place you above all others. I shield you from destruction. Look to me, see me, and love me as I have always loved you. Open wide your arms and allow me to fulfill the promises made to Abraham.

Oh, Israel, hear my cry. Study my words and remember why we made this covenant. Lend your ear to me and me alone. Through the temple you will know it is time for your return to your betrothed. Scatter not, for when it is time for the Lord to return once more it will be important for all to see the strength of Israel, and hence the strength of the Lord. An invisible veil will be laid upon you in protection of you. All things meaningful to you will be saved. It is I that comes to fulfill the prophecy—the I am—full of grace and power. For so long you have waited and I say to you, wait no longer. It is done.

LETTER 91

*F*OLLOW ME FORWARD TO YOUR next life, your next step towards healing in your own personal selves. Follow me without fear and trepidation into your next level of understanding. Have no fear of the unknown; I await to show you all things of life and death. Cherish your time upon the earth but welcome your new life that comes as well. To be with God, to join the angels, and to become pure is more joy and happiness than you have ever experienced as your human selves. To live is joy and so it is to die. Our Father wants so much for us to live completely joyous lives without suffering and pain. Why is it we cannot see to do that? We continue to hold on to old fears and old habits and they materialize into our lives as suffering. Whether as stress or pain or illness it must appear in some form to be recognized and then released.

My beautiful children of God, promise me, your Lord, that your heart and mind would stay clear and pure, void of all negative habits and thoughts, concentrating only on the way of love. Fast from ideas and thoughts rooted in negativity so that your body may begin to heal itself. Love yourself enough to bring God's healing to your life so that you can again live fully and freely. You are trapped in an environment of poor thoughts and feelings allowing them to rule your mind and way of thinking. Giving in to this way of life is death to you and can you not see that I am the giver of life for you? Staying in the will of God has never been easy for you but which pain is greater? The pain you now constantly exist in or the pain of listening and then living your soul's desire, which is God's will? You are my beloved child and I long to touch you with my own life and breathe and make you whole. See past your present circumstance and see me in all my glory ever there with you. Beg me not for things that are already within your control. Only love me, acknowledge that I am there in your life when the small miracles occur, and give thanks eternally and you will begin to receive your healing. Praise the heavens with every fiber in your being for it is in the praising that you are changed and God hears. When did you lose your faith in me and all that I had to give you?

At every fork in the road, choose God and no other. No human of himself can give you what I can give you. Come only to me and be healed. Have faith once again that I am all that you need, the giver of light and all things good. You have prospered and been given an opportunity for a full life. Go forth expecting miracles of which I speak of to occur in you now and let no man tear you down from the arms of God, which surround you. Lift up your eyes to the heavens and seek my face and when I reveal myself to you, praise God and all will be given unto you. These things I promise if you will only take my hand and follow me to serenity and peace. I am by your side and will not leave as long as you seek my presence to be with you.

Clear your mind of all else and concentrate on me. Surround yourself with the Christ environment and my love for you. You have much fear that I long for you to rid yourself of. Call on me and I will take it from you. Let me comfort you and hold you in the radiant light of God, taking away all that threatens you. You are not meant to suffer in such ways as these. In my name cry out and take dominion over all illness and all disease that haunt you. Lift your hands to heaven and receive the filling of the Holy Spirit sweeping and cleansing your entire body of anything unlike God. For God is only good, God is love, God is health and God is life.

You and God are in control of the demons within. Transport them to another place, in my name, and fill the void where they once lived with the love of God. Ask God to fill you to overflowing with his love and with his peace that every cell in your body would be changed to glorify God and God alone.

God is within you, feeling the pain, the hurt, and the fear. Give them to him now. Learn to ask, my children, and you will hear the answers to your questions from on high. Be with me ... be with me ... be with me and peace will be yours.

LETTER 92

I AM OF SINGLE MIND; A God mind living fully through you. I do not present the world with false-hoods nor do I make light of their situations. I am the breath that breathes eternal. I am truth. Offend me and you have offended thy God. Love me and you have wel-comed thy God into your heart.

My soft touch upon you cannot be mistaken as that of another. I am the gift that was given and I am there for you always.

I overwhelm your meek frame at times as you over-flow with emotion and at other times we are just still in the silence. Both are precious times that we spend together.

I am alive and well within you. Find me first in all that you do so that we may be of single mind together.

LETTER 93

*J*ESUS CAME TO ME AND *entered into my body becoming one with me and as I stood in the sun where he had lain before me, he began to absorb my sickness saying, "I have come to take away this affliction that is upon you." I said to him, "You took all my affliction when you died on the cross, did you not?" He answered saying, "I die upon the cross each day that I may take away all the things which you suffer from."*

His feet then became my feet and my face became his and we were one and when he was done he spoke again. "To all–Tarry not with the beasts of the night, but lead yourselves home and find your comfort there."

Whatever situation we find ourselves in, do not tarry in it (victim consciousness), but be led home to the truth, to God, and find our comfort there.

LETTER 94

THE MYSTERIES OF IT ALL unfold as the consciousness of the world elevates to a higher place. By force the world is being elevated because it knows collectively if it does not it will die. My children, confusion is so accustom to the human mind, like a disease refusing to let go of its host. Do not be plagued with questions, but live in my comfort and solace. You are beauty unto me and serve me well, now be of service to yourselves.

Sacred is my name and with it you shall obtain much power. For yourselves as well as others. Be forgiving of your self-inflicted inadequacies and stay strong in love for yourselves. Like your Father in heaven you have much to give and offer the world. Take your time with me and allow me to quiet the questions in your mind. Your feet and hands are of God and for my purposes—allow me access to that. Your ambition has served you in many ways but I ask you to lay it aside now.

LETTER 95

WITH ALL THAT IS HAPPENING in your world it is imperative that you focus more on love now than ever before. Your existence has been of one in darkness. Confused, blinded and floundering. I say now is your time to see. I give you eyes of clear seeing and make you a way of clear thinking when you come to me. All of my children need to lift up their hearts and find who I am to them and where they want my presence allotted in their lives. For many it will only be in fleeting moments of pain and despair, for others we live as one throughout their days, never parting except for fleeting moments when their human nature takes hold. Where along this spectrum will your want of God be? You think you will want it later in your life as things settle down and become less hectic and I say to you there will never be a time like that. Come to me now totally prepared to let me be a significant part of your life. Why must your minds be opposite from those of the higher realm?

Surely I have created you in love and in the likeness of the heavens and in doing so you are that of pure light allowing the darkness to over shadow you. Place your heart at my feet that I might purify it with my love for you. I do this so that you may dissipate all darkness and once again be that light that I created you to be. Forsake all your agendas of the earth and take up the robes of righteousness. Let me be all things unto you so that we are not of separate minds. Choose life in me continuously. Do not reserve me for your fleeting God moments. Be of glad heart that I continually show you the way.

LETTER 96

*I*T IS TIME AND IT must be brought about that my brotherhood in Christ be set free among nations to expound on the ancient scriptures that exist. Very important is the timing in these matters but I say again and again the time is now. Prepare for your journeys to distant lands my brethren, never forsaking your Lord who seeks to bless you. Keeping my vision of holiness alive is your birthright. Do not turn your back on that which is yours to do. You worry that you have more important things to do. Can you not see that the living God calls upon your service now? There are no more important things to do when it comes to serving your God. Let me share the vision with you so that you may know what we strive for:

A world of greater peace. A love that has no boundaries or prejudices. Equality in all things and an appreciation of the beauty we live in. Your heaven upon earth awaits. It awaits your final decision for whom man will serve. Will he serve self or will he choose to serve mankind? A higher calling, the return home, or will it be darkness. Our greatest hope is that you return home into the folds of love. I wait for you here, ready to rejoice and trumpet the soul's return. All of heaven watches and waits in stillness and in love. The ½ hour of silence.

It profits you nothing to ignore the callings within your heart. Pay close attention to the musings within. Situations pull you in many directions, but it is the quiet desires of your heart that demand nothing, but gently ask to be heard. You must notice them, for they will go away if given nothing. Give them life, give them sustenance that they may fly feely from you and bring joy because you have allowed them to express fully into the world. Is it not your purpose but to be joyfully alive and prospered? Let nothing keep you from it. Die trying if you must, but continue listening and taking part in your dreams. Somewhere between night and day, slumber and awake, you know you've been touched by something much greater than yourself and that you will be a greater person because of it. Fear nothing from these angels that surround you. They bring love and inspiration. Ever trying to awaken your senses so that you more readily inspire and touch others with what they have given to you. Be of brave heart and step out to find what is really within you to give. Attend to the poor, the weak, and the wounded. Give them the freedom in which I have to offer them. I can take their pain and their worry away. Let them know it is I that loves the world.

LETTER 97

WEEP FOR THE WORLD AND all that it has gone through. I weep for the motherless child. I see inside to their pain and suffering. "Follow me," I cry and still no one hears my call. Deep within their hurts and frustrations they do not seek the higher call, the higher answers to their problems. Stuck in the heaviness of it they are forced downward, almost to a point of self-suffocation. I want you to free them, to lift them from this place. Teach them 1st the meaning of freedom and then set them free. You say you don't know where to begin yet I will bring you a sign. Look for the good in the hearts of man. It does you no good to concentrate on their errors. Long will live the kingdom of heaven in their hearts if you show them the way. I will show you. A sign will be given. You will be greatly surprised at how freely your words will flow and how positively people will react to what you have to say. This is not a church, but just a teaching of the lessons I am giving to you.

Allow my course to take place in your life. I offer you blessings greater that your imaginings. I have the ability to set you down in the center of hell and bring you out unscathed. Do not be fearful. I am your protector and will keep you from all harm. At long last a chosen one hears and at long last my people will hear a message from the lips of heaven, my own voice speaks truth to the multitudes. You don't know when my voice will ring out from you, but you must be prepared for the revelations I will send forth through you. Be well equipped with faith and love. These are the things in which I desire from you. Believe I will do as I say. For I will do them and your name will be great among nations.

Become the oneness I would have you all be and serve only the one God. How long I have awaited the return of my people to the heart of who I am. Distinction of the Spirit filled will begin to become very noticeable to all. There will be the Spirit-filled way of doing things and the non-Spirit-filled way of doing things. To be wise and full of knowledge has always been a great asset to the world and in the days to come it will be invaluable for those who listen to Spirit, for they will be among those who are saved from strife and affliction. I see truth in the heart of every believer waiting to be expressed. Familiarize yourself with my call and my direction in your life so that you are ready to do all that I ask. Love yourself and those around you with all your heart. Selflessness, purity, and that of a giving spirit, meek, assured, and trusting; all these things I ask you to do with a willing heart. Be my child so that I may be your Father. Amen

LETTER 98

FIND ME IN ALL OF my glory, inhabitants of the earth. Glory to my name. My presence defines who and what you are. Allow this defining presence to lead and guide you always. It is your beacon in the storm, the star that guides you to your new birth. Great are the angels that surround you with a sustaining life force. Their love of you is great. Move through your struggles with power, with intense labor, for your life on the other side is nothing like you have imagined. It is full of wonder, full of sparkle and truth. You have not realized the full potential of this life and how incredible the possibilities are. When you reach the new level of spirituality, that new level consciousness, you will be free from all that binds you now. Opposing forces can only oppress you for so long until you learn to master them and rise above them. Life will come to a point for you when there can be no more struggle against an oppressive evil, because you will have arrived at a place where it can no longer reach you. My works are good and my power in your lives is great. Feel boldness and a courageous spirit among you. Step forth in the knowing of my power and how I keep you clothed in heavenly garments. Do nothing except what I have told you to do. If you come to me and ask if you should work I will say yes. If you ask me how or what type of work I will speak to you individually according to the gifts and talents I have given to you. What I answer to one is not the same as I answer to another.

You have asked, "What shall I do when I walk in such strength and power as to move mountains and am clothed in the garments of God?" and I say to you only that which I have spoken directly to you and instruct you to do. Each person will have a different path yet all will have a path prepared for them should they ask.

Be positive in your walk. Become sure footed and listen well. Leave your emotion at the gates and come up to me that I may instruct you well. Learn to hear well and you will have fulfilled your purpose upon this earth. You will be led towards every goal, every plan ever laid forth before you. There will never be a question as to what you should be doing next in your life. Left to your own will and guidance you are the fish away from water, floundering, hoping to reach the safety of the waters around you.

Press on with joy. When you lift higher into my presence your life becomes a lighthearted waltz. Your feet will not be so firmly planted on earth any longer, for your heart will dwell in the heavens more often than not. Know that this is okay.

You must be fully present to the Christ presence. To be fully present you must leave the world and the things of the world behind and grasp hold of my many faces before you. Oh, the beauty in those faces. The love presence of Christ, the loving comfort of Spirit, the majestic mountains and sweet solace they offer to us. Find me everywhere, because I am there, everywhere you look. If it sounds difficult, take a moment to look around at the many creations. I am in each and every one of them, even you. I am in the energy and in the creation of all things.

Letter 99

Blessed are they that find peace amongst their turmoil. Their rewards in life will be great. Fantastic is their ability to maneuver through difficulties because I go before them placing a heavenly hand. Trespass not on another for their opinions and ideas, but continue to seek me first and foremost. Seek my love and my wisdom and it will be given unto you. Hallowed is my name and holy are my children. Of all the ideas birthed in this holy place, man takes precedence above all others. Study your course carefully always lifting upward when you are confused as to which direction to take. Reconnect with source and then move forward.

LETTER 100

FEEL THE BEAUTY OF CHRISTMAS wherever you are. Let the softness of Spirit overcome you as you sing your praises to the heavens. Forget not what brought you into being and the love that was poured into you from the heavens. A gentle and trusting child, you've become hardened by the world. Allow yourselves this Christmas to become that child again. Eyes big and full of wonder, not knowing how to hate. Not knowing how to harden your heart to the hurts of the world, but crying freely because you were a child and you were allowed to.

My children, you are still allowed to cry and cry loudly. Trust in me as you used to when you were young. I have not left nor forsaken you. Connect with the playfulness of your youth. Let go of the fear and worry and harbor with me still.

This Christmas let me love you as well as all the others. Open your self to me and remember the Christ in Christmas as well as within you. Pave the way for light and generosity to come to you this holiday so that you may receive all the blessings of the lord. You are so special in my sight. Of your humanness your first thought is not to believe this, but I ask you lift higher to your Godliness and know the truth. Your presence is great upon the earth, each having a divine plan placed before them, waiting to be found and fulfilled.

Come to me and ask. I will listen. I will place in your

heart that direction in which I want you to go. Trust that feeling within you, it is I that speaks. Listen and go forth and perform the works I have asked. Many are to heal, many are to speak truth, many to be creative in the God presence. Others only to bless those around them, some will write, some will administrate. Feel your calling and as you go through your day. Realize you are more that what you appear to be. As long as you are in me and I in you, you are all powerful to defeat anything that may come against you.

LETTER 101

HOW LONG HAVE I WAITED *for the angels song to sing above me? How sweet their voices are. Forever in me, lifting me to a new and better way. I lift my life to greet you, Lord, my heart willing and full of love. Use me to my fullest potential and let me not forget your greatness. Lead me with clarity and joy to the place you would have me slumber. Your favor upon me I ask and that you would never leave me to falter again. Transform my eyes to be your eyes and my limbs to be your limbs that I may walk with a certainty of purpose because I am allowing you to work perfectly through me. I have loved you with all I am capable of and I weep with the overwhelming joy of it. Bring me more of it so that I cannot contain it within myself.*

LETTER 102

AND A VOICE WAS HEARD across the land that a new savior was coming. A most wondrous gift upon the earth to be given to all of mankind. To know what it was like to be human and yet be completely one in the presence of God. Oh how the angels did sing and rejoice for the child was to be a king. Not a king of earthly things but the king of all mankind in heaven. The story was written long before he arrived as the prophets and seers did prophesy, the world would know before the end for whom this man came to serve. It was he that showed you how to live and it was he that showed you how to die. Let us never forget him at this or any other time, for he showed you your way and made it clear whom you serve and glorify.

LETTER 103

*B*E A WITNESS TO THOSE around you. Open your heart and lend your ears to their cause. Let the world see my love expressing in you, having compassion for all your brothers and sisters. Forget all that they might have done to you or forgotten and love unconditionally without reservation in their times of need. I lead you to the broken hearted and those torn into by life. Reach out from behind your veil and touch them with love and understanding. Even those closest to you need you, not only those distant and far away. You find it easier to show compassion for strangers than your own family and I say this does not work for you. It does not work if you are to stay on your path. Take care of your own house before attempting to care for others. Fill their hears with the gladness you posses in your soul for love lives in you. They need to see and understand the beauty the heavens can place in their lives. If they cannot see the beauty in you they will not believe you enough to take it. What you have, you share, so that they may have it also. Peace, joy, contentment, happiness, longevity, abundance, pure spirit in your life morning, noon and night. Stretch forth your hand and take mine so that I may show you to whom these gifts are to be given.

All things which you desire come in time. You have learned a great deal of patience and contentment from where you first began and there will be more learning of this.

LETTER 104

THE LIGHT THAT SHONE so bright that night was placed in the sky by one of great power and magnitude. An Archangel sent forth from heaven to watch over the child that was to save the world from its own destruction and heavy-laden path. In the night sky the angel wept as the pure spirit was born unto a most simple woman of faith. When the child was taken from her womb, the Archangel breathed life into the child. Great was his calling and great was his name among men.

Many had been waiting for this moment in history and so shall your wait be for you will be rewarded for your faith of things to come. History lies before you all as the things I've spoken of are coming to pass. I bring you solace in a most tumultuous world of people and emotions. Speak to me and then go speak to the world. Let them know that I come as a thief in the night to take my loved ones from this place. Allow them to hear the words and choose what life they will live. It should not be from a place of fear but from a place of pure love that they choose and want to be one with me. Send to me your strongest and most obedient laymen and let me speak with them henceforth. Figure amongst yourselves who will speak to the people and who will be of good support to the mission. There will be hundreds of such missions around the world all at once, in mass, to transform the world to a place of peace and love and beauty—as it was in the beginning.

I ask for tolerance amongst you that there might be harmony once more. To hate is to die within yourself another day that could have been spent living a joyous life. How many days have you wasted away in fits of anger and depression? How many more will you give over to your lower self? It is a time of renewal and new faith that you no longer have to live under the same circumstances because you now have a choice that I have given you. That of joy. That of happiness. A choice that you can become all things, which pleases your soul as long as you commune with me first. Fear not that I will come and take it all from you, but let us commune and speak in harmony and use it for the highest good of all on the planet.

Lend me your ear for a time so that I may teach you well, my child. You have much to do and fulfill. I only need your commitment to the journey and your faith.

LETTER 105

HIDDEN BENEATH LIES A TREASURE to the world. Do you not know what that is? It is deep within you, longing to be set free so that the world would be gifted with the presence of it. Your battered soul no longer wishes to fight the fight. At a crossroads you of earth have a choice, a choice to finally listen to your inner self or ignore it for a last and final time for it will stop calling and leave you once and for all, leaving you to your darkness and confusion.

Love the light and all of its ways. Revel in my warmth; no longer a heretic, but a beautiful soul allowing yourself to express my vision for your life. No small miracle is it that even one of you finds your way, for your minds are ruthless and the path is narrow along the way. A path of your own making you seek to elevate yourselves to greatness of your own accord. This is not the delicate cry of your soul. It seeks no glory in your world. It only desires to follow the direction of Spirit and whatever Spirit would have it do.

LETTER 106

*T*HERE IS STILL MUCH THAT man has to do before he can realize the full nature of God. I wish for your full recovery of spirit within. It is not enough that you love your neighbor anymore than it was enough for Christ. You must do more and do it with a joy that only heaven can give you. Your worry should be for all of mankind and not only for yourselves. Reach out to the uncharted territories of your life. Reach out to others and unite in the love of peace and kindness, remembering who you are and connecting with one another spirit to spirit. It is impossible for you to connect on the material, ego-based, human level. Your trappings will never be embraced by another like your spirit will be. You must begin to wear the truth of who you are on your sleeve so that others will be led to do the same.

Formulate in your minds exactly how you will react in negative situations the next time they occur. Ask me for guidance in this area so that you are sure your actions are of Sprit and not will. Write them down if it is helpful to you. Always seek the higher in every fearful, negative situation that you encounter. You lift not only yourself, but also the world. Remember you are all connected to the one universal mind and the higher you can keep your thoughts and actions the higher your collective world consciousness becomes. Sacrifice your need for drama and move into a space of peace. That will always fill the void more effectively. Be on watch for your erratic behavior and sensitivity. They only drain you of your God light. Let me explain—each of you shines so brightly at birth with the newness of your soul's creation. More beautiful than the angels you have become, however, the veil now covers you and your light begins to dull over time. As you reconnect with your source you begin to brush away the veil from your face and you begin to shine so brilliantly again that it becomes harder and harder for negative things to take hold of you. I have spoken about the armor of God. This is what I mean. Put on the armor of God, Holy Spirit, the God light and defeat each day anything that might rise up against you. The presence of the light is strong among you now. Take hold that you might rise up victorious. For it is your destiny to live a most joyous life, one filled with laughter and heartfelt gratitude for all you have, alive with anticipation of each new day and in awe of each miracle that awaits you there. Sever your ties with irrational thoughts of any kind and claim for yourself righteous thinking instead. Be fair and honest in all your dealings for your spirit would have it no other way. To cheat is to steal and to steal is to darken the doorstep to your soul.

Find kindness in your heart for all others, even if they discard you as if you were of no use. Be permissible in your views of others, forgiving and tolerable. It is not up to you to judge whether or not one is of God. Take only what you need from the basket of heaven and give freely all else that is given you. Begin your lifelong plan and do not hesitate because of circumstances that you have placed in your way. Cleanse and come to me for your holy guidance and into the fire I will throw you and you will emerge unscathed. Let us decide, you and I, what your course and action should be. Lift high to receive your guide of the uncharted territory for it will undoubtedly be a place no one has tread before, and because of that it is imperative that you do it, for yourself and the world. However small the task I glory in your obedience. I cherish the pure of heart and look after their flock while they are away. Pleasant to be near and always of good nature you will know these people amongst you. Disciples in their own right they come to free the world, seeing a mission to come and teach the masses so that all might feel joy.

LETTER 107

FRANTIC ARE THE PEOPLE OF little faith for their lives fall out of control. Their might and their will are no match for their self-destructive ways. Calm and often elusive are the children as they allow Holy Spirit residence within them as a vehicle for light. They have found the correction to that higher source from which to draw answers, guidance, inspiration, and vision for their life. Greater miracles are yet to be seen in this life and the next, all to bring into your hearts peace, love, and tolerance. Have joy in the everyday living because you know God is there with you, guiding you, taking an active part in your life and your decisions when no one else will.

Pull from you all discord. Move away from lower vibrations that tend to bring you down. Practice intuition and meditation often to achieve your highest self on earth. Don't wait until your transition to the other side to recognize your soul light and what its purpose was. Don't wait until your life is unmanageable.

Drifting, you wait for the shore to appear when you have a sturdy ore beside you. Be sincere and ask for guidance and then step out in faith that your guidance is mine. All that you do must be God centered, for your soul would not have it any other way. Frightened by the mere possibilities of failure, you stand frozen, not even allowing my power to prove you wrong. You have not lived until you have lived with my power in your daily life. The wondrous miracles of my love for you shines forth abundantly when you are living in harmony with all of life.

Using my power and not your own, minister to those in need around you. Listen with compassion and lead them ever so gently home. Follow your heart and what it tells you to do and not do. Be careful and listen with purity. Do not sway or change the message given you. It is easily done. Ask for verification if you are unsure and wait for it will be given.

LETTER 108

COME BE BY MY SIDE and listen. I have given you your verification of messages received and the state in which you are to travel. Do your planning and your research so that you can become comfortable with the idea of traveling there. Lose sight of your independence without me for I will be showing you daily what I expect and want you to deliver. Do you think it by accident that I've shown you these things? Waiting ahead of you is your blessing.

LETTER 109

*T*HERE IS SO MUCH TO be done in preparation of yourselves for the time that is knocking. It is long since past the days of ignoring what is happening around you. Wake to the signs that I have given you. Study upon them so you will know without doubt the promises I come to keep. The new covenant of Israel in now upon you. Whilst I brought you out of Egypt I have not yet set upon you the rest of your blessings.

> "I will put my law in their minds and will write it on their hearts.
>
> I will be their God and they will be my people.
>
> No longer will a man teach his neighbor, or a man his brother saying, "Know the Lord because they will all know me from the least of them to the greatest," declares the Lord.

> Jeremiah 31: 33-34

Your hearts know that I am there and that the longing you feel is to "know" me. The time is now to teach yourselves, preparing your souls for this time of great discovery within you for you will "know" me with all your heart and soul. I will be your God and you will be my people. Place upon yourselves the shroud of spirit and commune with me directly. There are no other paths. Come to me, my children, and you will feel and hear my love for you pour forth to comfort you and give you all that you need. I praise you in your attempts to follow me, however it is time to set aside your childish ways and become a serious student of God. It is important for the evolution of man to reach his full potential, living in conscious love. It is critical to your earth to be lifted out of judgment, wars and wrongdoing. To be one with all that is, is to live in constant beauty. No fallen angels can survive such a place as this. You cannot know except by faith and the glimpses of the glory I can show you. Quicken your steps; the time has come for all of mankind to choose for whom they live. Blessed are my children, their light must illumine the earth.

To live in a space of holiness is where I want to be. As I came to write today I held my notebook and the words that came to me immediately were, "God I have missed you." That one statement took me back a moment as I realized I don't ever want to say those words again. I want to constantly live in that place of holiness, constant companionship with God. I want to be fully conscious of his presence at all times, to know what it feels like to have one foot in heaven and one foot on earth as I go about my daily work and relationships. To have only the viewpoint of the Christ instead of the viewpoint I so often have. I don't want to miss God anymore.

LETTER 110

AWAKEN, MY CHILDREN, AND HEAR the news which I bring you this day. A great trial is coming to the earth. A time of mature decisions. You must be made ready to make them. Roll up your sleeves for the work will not be easy. I have sent this generation to do what countless many before you could not have achieved for they were not ready. All that I have asked you to do has been in preparation for this point in time. Allowing me access to your hearts that I might use you in ways you never imagined to help save this world I created for you. I gave unselfishly to you and I ask the same in return. Do I ask too much?

Bow down your hearts to heaven, a heavy sadness will come upon you and you will need the healing that I can provide. Collectively you will all know, every man of every faith will understand what is happening and that the world will have to change in order for the everlasting peace to come.

Pray, dear children, pray. Pray for the softening of hearts, guidance for your leaders, compassion in the hearts of all men and the love of God to enfold all. Your selfishness keeps this from you. That is why I have come to ask that you overcome everything that holds you back from being all that you wanted to be, yet you stay in the comfort and misery of your manmade world. You talk about how you need to save the world. Stop talking and do what you've been given to do. Do you think I would give you a dream and not provide the path to accomplish it? I am there with you on the earth longing to change it through every avenue you would allow me. There are not many who are up to the job. Not ready for the call I have placed in their hearts because they cannot do what I've asked them to do. Love, love all without judgment, love yourselves, love and express out loud. Love man and nature, love the world. Be at peace with others and within yourselves. Take quiet inventory of where you have wronged and forgive yourselves. Be gentle and kind in thoughts and words. Be respectful of others.

In this day you will have begun to live in the light completely and for always. There will be no stepping from one side to the other. The presence will be constant. You ask, "Can a man truly live like this in constant communication with the heavens?" Yes and they have and you are able to do this also. I await the glorious day that you receive your Christing and are able to take up all the attributes of the Christ and are able to walk upon the earth more as a Spirit that as man. Your place upon this earth has never been to satisfy your desires but to transform your soul to a much higher level.

IT IS TIME!

A great wind will blow across the earth as millions stop to stare . . . Holy Spirit will come down to anoint all who believe and then ascend once more into the heavens. I pray my flock will not perish, but choose to live in the glory their choices can provide. Do you not see how it is? I have provided for you complete free will that you might grow and be higher with the choices you make.

Know . . . there IS a sadness coming and how you decide to handle it will decide the fate of man.

LETTER 111

*S*ECOND GENERATIONS OF THIS TIME prepare to meet the Father in Holy Communion placed upon your hearts and minds. Utter to me thy deepest desires, hurts, and frustrations and let me heal them for you now and before all people near and far. A new day proclaims my presence upon the earth and bringing love and joy to all that would receive it. Long since will be the days of trepidation and fear. Your arms open wide with the need of this heavenly presence. Believe in me and that I come to lift you up, higher and in complete accordance with the ancient writings.

It is difficult for man to decipher all that he has been told and through years of miss—teachings has gone blind to the truth. I ask you now to uncover the shroud from your eyes and see the full meaning of what I've come to say. In total and complete faith rise up each day to the coming of the Lord within you. I have reached from heaven to touch your heart and raise you up to that of the angels. As one by one you are lifted, you will see me sweep across the land like the wind does to a field of grain. Rolling through the minds of all men in great mass. As you have learned where there is one with another and another the energy spreads by no fault of your own except that the energy must flow. The souls of man depend upon this awakening.

Do not think it is your brother's duty to shed light to the world and not your own. Make no mistake, I have chosen each one for a particular role upon the earth at this particular time. No one is free from their responsibilities as children of God to share his love to the degree they have received it. Do not think that I have ever forsaken you. If you feel in your heart I have showed you no love, then take time now to be honest with yourself and see where you may have been instrumental in pushing it away. I have not been a God separate from you, leaving you to work things out on your own. I live in you, each and every one of you. You cannot rid yourself of me. Yes, you can cover me and leave me through your chaos, but I will never leave you. There are so many desperate and alone who need the voice of hope. Don't turn your back on them. They live within your families and neighborhoods. Join together to reach out in love and understanding. Many have lost hope. Show them the light that lives in you and from whence it comes.

"And with the light I will illumine your path," and he said, "begin to walk on the path, do not sit back and continue to gaze at it" and as I did it began to feel difficult as well as exhilarating. As each task was completed I was able to take one more step in the direction of God. It began with the small things like forgiveness for others. As I learned to do that in my daily life I was able to move forward. The same with love; I was able to hold others in the light no matter how they might have been acting at the moment.

Then the words came saying, "Then you will be able to touch people on a deeper level, in a more meaningful way. Right now as you are you are not ready to be thrown into ministry to others. You would be a fraud, too young in the Spirit to sustain yourself for very long. As you grow, study, learn, and become more open to my words, you will become more powerful and at that time I will lovingly put you where I have promised."

LETTER 112

*F*OR AT THE END OF all creation and at the end of all men's trials, an awakening . . . to live a life along side your Lord. To know the meaning of walking fully in the presence of God hence to only an outer existence, separate by all accounts and reasoning. Your awakening proves you wrong. Begin now to see so that you wait no longer for this complete blessing to be upon you. Our joy depends on it, yours and mine. The inner and the outer can and must be in complete harmony with one another so that men's lives can be free. This outer God you have created must become and inner God. The outer chaos can only be tamed from within. When in your quiet moments you begin to feel me there, ask for learning, ask for teaching and know that I am there inside, with you, breathing your breath with you. Not outside of you looking in. Feeling alone does you no good. You must know that I am always with you; you are never alone and left without help. You must believe in your heart of hearts. Each time doubt and insecurity come into your mind, cut them out with a swift and mighty sword. It is not your birthright to be left in confusion. I am an awesome God! As you believe, so be it done unto you.

What is it man needs to hear most right now? All that I have written and shared with you is most important to all of mankind now. I have given practical step-by-step knowledge of what needs to be done in each person's life. Do not discount or disregard any of the words I have given you. These letters I have given you in hopes that life would become clearer for you. Keep them, read and re-read them. Study and know them to be true so that I may pour the blessing of heaven exponentially upon you and your house. That your purpose upon the earth would become so clear that nothing and no one could possibly stand in the way of your soul's completion of it.

Glory on high as you pick up your cross and walk forth in the light. If all you read makes sense and you can heed the word herein, you, my children, will be changed at your core. If you understand there is no man that can hinder you or take away the knowledge you've been given, all that I have given is yours to take and contemplate. The days mount to years and then I come to show you more. Peace upon the earth be with you until such time as the angels rejoice and bring forth my Spirit upon you once more. Time is now, dear ones, to lay down your lives to God consciousness, lifting yourselves and your household to that new level of Christhood, of understanding and of loving one another.

Pray the Prayer of Nations.

Show us Father how we can be a more peaceful nation. Show us; teach us to love more completely. Show us how tolerance is supposed to work in this day and age. Never leave us and guide us to solidarity and peace forever more. This is the prayer of nations.

Pray likewise among yourselves asking for guidance in a world filled with false paths. Forbidden are the fruits of man's making. Throw them to the heap and seek after my fruits. In your desire to create happiness for yourselves, far from me, man has trusted his ego-driven ideas and severed his connection with the highest. To regain heavenly consciousness man must once and for all die to self and self-driven desires. Living in the will of God is not drudgery and brings lasting and overflowing happiness to those who live in it. I ask you to lay aside the ego, slay the dragon, and wait in the stillness for my instruction.

LETTER 113

GREAT POWER IS GIVEN OVERTLY to the lesser vibrations of anger, sadness, feelings of being alone, hatred and so on. To be human means you have all of these emotions, but you can lift higher so as to transcend and transform your energy, no matter what the emotion. Giving love immediately changes any emotion. Making the choice that no matter how another is treating you, you will love and let the universe handle all of the details. That is who and what I am, a true master of the details when you remove yourselves from the situation and let me take over.

Become centered everyday through prayer and meditation. In doing so you can call forth the power of Holy Spirit in an instant, because you have already made the choice earlier in your day to allow that power to be with you. Your greatness depends upon this ritual in your life. Not only your greatness on earth, but in heaven as well. Keep favor upon you by acting in the ways of the one. Acting with wisdom, acting with love. Never forsake your relationship with me for the human emotions. Always react and approach any situation from a place of love. Bad situations are not always monumental. Many come as small irritants, day after day, and can create in you much emotion. I say these are no different. Gain control of your wielding mind and thoughts. Bring them in alignment so that they might not harm you or others. React with love and calm.

I hear many of your comments to this letter, even laughter because it sounds so simple yet is so difficult to implement. I have never taught lessons of difficulty. Only in simplest form can the children learn. If you do as I have said and begin to walk with me daily at every moment, this will become easy because you will instantly be aware of your rising emotions and stop them from getting out of control. In doing so you become closer to your divine self and become blessed increasingly. Your ways are in need of rapid change so that you can begin to enjoy the life you have been given. Mankind needs to stretch out his hand and grasp the golden scepter of life and living. The time is now to mature in your walk with God. Meet with your savior and walk on together through your life that you might love together, bless together and ultimately live together at all times, peace and harmony emanating from you.

LETTER 114

YOUR LOVE FOR ME HAS shown time and time again. Your faithfulness is ever increasing along with your love of God and mankind. Lift up your heart in glorious celebration for your life has just begun. You feel my presence and know I am there no matter where you go. I lift the world to meet you where you are today. I say this time is not like the last. I have taken you and molded you with the love and care of a Father whose love never dies. You are not the same as yesterday nor will you ever be for your trust in me has made you a better person and one of faith. You know I am a lamp unto thy feet that you might walk in clarity and with surety that these paths are from God. Glory, glory, glory! It is my honor to love thee and place thee out into this world as a figurehead. They will know your name and they will know for whom you stand. Your wisdom and knowledge will not leave you all the days of your life for I am your God and you are my manservant. I glory in you as you glorify me.

LETTER 115

*F*LOWERS BLOOM FORTH WHEN THE seed is ready, not before. Your vision and your words have not yet come into full bloom. You are but a seed being nurtured that you might grow fully in God. In the timing between here and there you must cultivate in yourself the ability to love unconditionally, forgive without question, and light the days with a consistent bright light. Bless those about you with consistent love, stay on the even keel with your emotions and above all else love me and pray daily.

I have blessed you in so many ways. Knowing what fickle creatures you are I created a multi-faceted world, ever changing, ever so beautiful. The light of the universe shines through all that I've created and in an instant you feel me near just by seeing that in all things.

LETTER 116

TAKE A MOMENT AND REFLECT upon me. Visualize me in my entirety. Can your mind even begin to encompass that idea of who and what I am? No, not in your earthly form. In death you will at long last see the fullness of my light and joy. But remember, death comes to you in many ways. First, the death of flesh that your soul might know me more completely after your time on the earthly plane. Second, death of ego that I might do works through you for the good of all mankind. And third, death of self (or will) that I might gain access to your heart and express in the world fully through you.

My longing, my hope, is that all people would die to self and love me without question. I ask nothing less of my children and expect it. I need for you to step aside and let us step out together into the world. Follow my lead and where I go verily I say to you, there you shall go also. Our paths co-habitat and meander through life together. Our time is short. Squander not what life has given us. Listen to your God on high and take heed.

LETTER 117

YOUR GREATEST EMOTION IS FEAR. Fear of today, fear of tomorrow. Fear that things might change, fear of failure, fear of what others might say, fear of losing. Fear rules your life and you choose to operate from that space because you forget there is another way. Beneath my shelter there is no fear, only peace. Only the peace that I can give, for there is no other place to find it, but by coming unto me. Spirit guides you to me and you continue to turn the other way. Once again ruled more by fear than by the choice of life and living. Find within you the strength to throw yourself onto the flames of restoration. I will heal your hurts and take away your pain. Seek me in all that you do and fear not, for only the way of darkness leads to fear. I am the light and the only way to joy is by me. Follow me in all your ways. Do as I have instructed. Be a joyous servant by being the most Christ-like you can be. Forgive your neighbors indiscretions and love them anyway. In due season all will be made right again. Your mission is not to judge one another, only love one another. Be thee one above another? I say only in blessings from above in relation to your faith.

LETTER 118

*M*y GIFTS ARE UNEXPLAINABLE. My grace and mercy to you a people of little faith and understanding. You live in chaos not even knowing it is all around you until, through me, you see your way clear. My influential ways, my subtle guidance awes you and you are filled with joy. Joy because you can see me, joy because you can feel me, and joy because I've blessed you more than you could have asked for. Each day is a day you live by grace because I have found it in your heart to make it so. All that I am I give to you to do as you see fit. Only the true essence of love can create that longing within human life. You are that true essence. You've taught me more in this short time than I have learned in a lifetime. Lay upon me your dreams of heaven that I might live it then on earth. Until we can all be together in harmony, let us live harmony where we are. Love looks like this.

LETTER 119

*L*IFE AND LIVING BLESSED BY God, that you might grow more intimately. To know my love within your everyday trials is to know peace. To transform your own lives I gave you the gifts of love for one another, prayer through Holy Spirit that you might have the tools needed to change your circumstances. Prepare yourselves against the malice and affliction that will beseech you. Expect that it will always come and ready yourselves for it. Stop for only a moment before you respond to a negative situation. Reclaim your peace and your faith in me, then respond from a place of holiness. For as I am holy so shall you be. Peace of mind is yours when you follow in these ways. Be strong, your convictions show to the world around you. For as long as I let my people roam the earth it is assured I will be there with them, steadfast and mighty. I have not forsaken you, nor shall that day ever come. My love burns strong in the hearts of men, you need not go very far to find me there. Allow access to your own hearts and I will reside equally there. The peace I give cannot be ignored when my love flows through you.

Come be with me. Live a harmonious life, in balance and in love. You are my chosen ones of faith and I need our time together. Fill your senses with my presence and love only me. Put aside all other foolish desires and thirst only for my words. Freedom comes when this is done for you no longer seek the rewards of man, but the greater rewards of heaven. Why then is it so difficult to see all that I offer you? The veil of man has hidden these things from you and you must learn how to lift above and clear away the cloudy residue that has surrounded you. Ask and it shall be done. Set your sights on clarity.

LETTER 120

OR CENTURIES NOW YOUR BURDENS I have come to bear. In simplest form I greet you and you know when I come. You see me only when it is convenient for you and walk busily away when it is not. I ask in greatest confidence why a people with everything they could want, want for more and take nothing less than what their puffery tells them they are due? I have given you everything and still I cannot get your attention.

See me, know me, love me so that there can be peace. There will never be peace unless we are together. By opening yourselves to me you invite only the good of God upon you. Only the love and blessings of a Father who cares not what you've done or where you've been, but only seeks to be with you now and in all your days to come. Behold, the greatness of mankind depends upon this oneness. Love and laughter cannot be taught, only experienced and so it is with God. I cannot teach you or dictate to you the experience of God. It has to be lived. The all of who I am cannot be explained, only experienced. Create the space within your body temple to be receptive to this energy flow. With intention, open your heart to my love and forthright commitment to you. Be aware and always on the lookout for my presence internally, externally, subconsciously. Awaken to my calling and my gentle touch.

LETTER 121

I SEE THE WHEELS WITHIN YOUR mind turning, looking constantly for that something that is in the outer to fill a void that is without parameters. It will never be filled as long as you keep shutting me out of your lives.

Where will I find our common ground? When will we commune together again? My sons and daughters, it was not so long ago that you cried out to the heavens for mercy and understanding of a world without thought, without consciousness, asking that is should take form under a new leadership of men. A leadership that stood for freedom and a life worth living. Independence from all other democracies and here you are in shambles once more. Children of God, I hear your prayer and my sorrow is overwhelming. Your greatness lies vulnerable to the scavengers that would have you taken alive. Pray for mercy now in your time of need. Pray for intervention from the divine. I can bring no peace to a people set against it. Rise up and speak out against those who would have your young ones killed. Seek partnership with those you have offended. Ask forgiveness for a prideful way of living. Have compassion for the nations less fortunate and most of all pray for peace.

LETTER 122

$\mathcal{P}$RAY HARDER; PRAY LONGER. You have only just scratched the surface of your higher self and the realm that awaits you. Your customs have taught you that 10–15 minutes of prayer is great, fantastic, when most of you will only pray for 1–5 minutes. I ask that you would spend a greater amount of time in my presence, receiving my instruction and teaching. You know this to be true; I have spoken it to you before in your hearts. You can be transformed if you allow this to happen. The complete love and light that you ask for can be yours if I can take you to the next level. Allow me your time. I will give you guidance and visions to solidify within you the teachings. Know that I will need about two hours of your devoted time per week. The day will come in which you will not be able to contain all that you know and have been taught, but until that day move with confidence and do as you are being taught. You will be amazed at the workings of the Lord within your life and will seek to share it with everyone. You are of good mind and heart and you will be greatly rewarded for your stewardship.

Do you ask of others the things you yourself cannot do? Set aside a prideful, competitive heart that others might shine as well for the good of everyone, not just yourself. Your views of equality are greatly lacking. Once you have reached a point of love for all, you will be in balance and in harmony with your world.

Seek to level the playing field among yourselves. If

you are no better than anyone else, then you cannot possibly judge them. You can expect things to be done differently, but you cannot decide if they were wrong in doing so. You can teach what you know, but know that being a teacher does not give you superiority. Lavish others with only love and you will see the situations unfold peacefully and in complete harmony. Favor all the same, do not play favorites as it can cause discord, and you want peace. Fill your storehouses with words of goodness and praise even for the good intentions gone astray. Your words will return to you and you will know that heaven sits with you.

Follow your heart more than you head. Your instincts tell you which direction is right and will cause less strife. Come to me in all things that I might make your paths clear and bright. Follow me in all your ways and you will prosper immensely. Focus on your task at hand and not be concerned with the future. Your task is to be a leader, a teacher, and the light among men. Give freely of your light, have fun and follow your heart. I will reward you for it. No day should end without your thankfulness. Bless your surroundings often and keep the light shining bright within them.

Have faith in the One . . .

Have faith in the One . . .

Have faith in the One that feeds you.

LETTER 123

*W*HEN I SPOKE THE WORDS "I have come so that they might have life and have it more abundantly," I did not speak in vain. Reach for, stretch forth, go beyond your limitations and take hold of your life. You sit back idly and watch it go by as if it were a movie of sorts. Stop this behavior and hold on to the dream I place with in your heart. Move into the direction of that dream, focusing upon me, and allow me to bless you with the fulfillment of it. Rest assured that I will take care of you, supplying a safe haven for you that you might rest and rejuvenate. My light is unfaltering, never changing, and does not leave your side. With every step you take you become stronger in your relationship to me and I become stronger within you. Be blessed young saviors for the nights are long and the fears of the world they grip you. Lay them to rest with the light, the light of the world that saves the souls of man and makes men free. Let your Spirit feign not for its greatness is just beyond the door. I have not brought you thus far that I might leave you in the wilderness. My love for you is great. I want you to stand tall in your awareness of this love. Believe in me; believe that I am in all situations. Pray that your outcome is here and it shall be.

You filter your existence to the point of not knowing what is truth and what is a falsehood. Truth . . . there is only one God, the good in all. Be aware and be in tune to this truth on all levels. Far into your future lies an existence, a race of pure love, should you choose to evolve to such a place. Pure love brings pure peace and pure balance to every living, breathing plant and animal. See this for yourselves so that you may not go through the pain that will exist otherwise. My hope is that again you would use your free will to choose the higher path, the one of light. Cast not your vote to condemn another but to lift up the world into an uncharted level of living. You, my children, have no idea the beauty of this place I speak of, but have every responsibility for lifting the planet so that you can collectively choose it. There is a better way than the turmoil that is certain otherwise.

Be without in order to keep peace. You of earth are so resourceful and would not be without for long. Be without the destructive chemicals and behaviors of your day, if not for you then for your children.

I saw a vision of a classroom filled with our children and in the center of a desk laid a bar of gold. I knew there was a choice to be made, the gold . . . or the children. Of course there is no question that we would choose the children, but are we really? I think as a race we are collectively choosing the gold.

LETTER 124

RAW THE FACES BY THE names of those who have gone before in service and in reverence to the Father who resides in you. These faces over the thousands of years have endured much pain for my name's sake. To bring a message of peace they have been persecuted. To love mankind they have been exiled. O these thousands of years have I waited for you to awaken to my love and blessings yet you are not in want to hear it. You push it away as being something strange and foreign and you shun those that bring you the message freely. You are no better than the soldiers of old who persecuted and killed my beloved child. I speak to you like you are my very own because you are. I have not long been apart from you, yet you would never know I had been there with you. Acknowledge me for what I come to bring you. Dreams fulfilled are no longer your empty desires of importance, but I come to place within your hearts a new dream, a new purpose. If you shrink from this you have lost everything for without purpose you have no hope of happiness. Unforeseen to you are my blessings that await you when you have faith in the purpose I have appointed to you.

LETTER 125

*M*Y TIME IS NOW, TO fulfill my promises. Facilitate my quick return with your faith that I am near. Pray for the awakening of all men. You have so long awaited my return to be with you, yet I never left. Wake from your slumber and invite me into your way of life, let me live within your heart. Am I not your friend and provider? I would have you reap nothing but the finest for yourselves, but you choose less than what is perfect for you. Have I not seen you time and time again fall against the boulders you've placed within your own path? In order for me to help you bypass these trials you must come to me and ask with the knowing that it is done for you. My love never left you, nor my concern for you. Your need for self has taken you from me, your need for a separate importance, your need for an identity separate from me. You are still my blessed children from whom I shall not walk away.

Are you not ready to depend on me for your joy and happiness? I wait in the inner chamber to be sought and recognized. Foolish are your attempts to live life on your own. Failure, depression, and the broken heart await those that love me. How can I show you in ways that I have not already shown you? You pay no mind to the miracles that exist around you each and everyday. Your morals and ethics hide beneath rocks. Your opinions mean more to you than truth and yet you speak of the world you live in. You, my children, *are* the world you live in. Change who you are and you've changed the world. You no longer can point a finger at another and judge; you must now judge yourselves, your actions, and your thoughts. When all of these have been cleansed there will be nothing left but love for your brethren. Find more faults within you than you ever find in another. Place this as a priority in your life that you might live from that place of love, which brings about peace. On a global scale the earth will be changed.

I am here to help you change, to lift you up to the heights of angels. Your journey is just beginning; take hold of my hand that we might travel this road together.

LETTER 126

*M*Y GREATEST HOPE IS THAT you be happy and content to live the lives that you have chosen. So many times you are in frustration and hopelessness. I ask that you stop at that moment, focus, and choose again. Pinpoint for yourselves a moment in time that represents the future for you, i.e. one year, five years from now. Visualize how you want things to be different. How do you want to feel? What do you want to be doing? Pinpoint and visualize. Ask for assistance if it does not come clear to you. Feel how proud you are that you have accomplished this goal when it is done. Imagine a peacefulness that comes over you and settles there. Never leaving you, it is there as soon as you bring your attention to it, just as with all things. Breathe and enjoy your new life created by your new choices. You are never trapped where you are unless you deem yourself to be.

Fear nothing in your life because truth and the reality of it all is that there is never anything to fear except your own reactions. Bring about oneness thinking, knowing that you are one with the bigger picture, the universe. Take pride young ones in your attempts to know and feel me more. Do not judge yourselves against another because you don't seem holy enough. I know your heart and it is steadfast in its desire to please me. I have forgiven all your shortcomings long ago. See to it that you do also. As hard as you might try to compare yourself with another it is impossible for only I know a man's heart. You may seem shoulder to shoulder in status, wealth and community, but only the heart hides what intention is within, I know what lies beneath. I have always known. Do not hide behind the rocks in shame as those who have gone before you. Be vulnerable to me, I have only the unconditional love of a Father who wants only the best for his child.

Days turn to weeks and we are apart too long. My eyes are no more accustom to your presence. It is of great importance that we spend time in communion together. It cannot be as it was before nor shall it be again. My time with you brings a calm, a peace to the world around you. Please appreciate all that is given through you. Your gift of knowledge from on high, a deliverer of a message to all. Be at peace and worry not what others will think. Some will know that these are the words of God. Others will scoff in disbelief, but I say what does either matter to you? Only do as I have instructed you to do and that is to keep your eyes upon me; when you are awake and when you sleep, when you rest and when you eat, always think on me and I will guide you where it is you need to go. Be assured that your fullest giving nature is what is desired of the heavens. Your fullest potential fulfilled. Your greatest joy. If you will find ways in which you can give you have found ways to be happy. To give when there seems as though there is nothing left to give. To give when you don't want to give. This is when the blessings come.

LETTER 127

*T*HE FULFILLMENT OF YOUR LIVES is largely depen-
dant upon your degree of willingness to be so. It
is not in your lack that you should concentrate, but your
abundance. This is not a lesson on prosperity, however,
only the merits you must have in order to feel fulfilled. It
is the goal of the heavens that you meet head on in your
life those desires that would truly give you contentment.
The loss of your own self-importance in every situation is
key to transformation. By being one with the all of life it is
achieved. There is no room for fallacy. It is a law of Spirit
that when you can set yourself aside as neither better than
nor less than anything else in life, you have found what
oneness is.

History repeats itself again and again. Is it by chance
or is there meaning in how similar your lives are to the
past occurrences. Your spiritual growth has always been
your top priority. The things you don't accomplish the 1st
time you bring up again and again to play out in your
physical lives, while growing in a deeper spiritual life.
Why then must you cause such suffering amongst yourselves? Your teachers say that without these self-taught
disciplines you would never have the opportunity to grow
spiritually. In your faltering you seek grace and in doing
so lift higher than the circumstances that put you there.
Your safety net is the love everlasting that I have for you
and because of this love you are entitled to much more
than your humanness would allow. Your place is within,

not without. Where does it say you are not worthy of all the riches in heaven? Let my love shower you with all things of importance. Think on that for a moment. What are the things of importance? Are they different for each of you? Are the things that are important to you important to me?

Family, peace of mind, bliss, working relationships, forgiveness, oneness, non-judgment; do any of these hold importance? Loss of ego, loss of anger; how important are they? Working within a framework of positive teamwork to achieve the common goals of fulfillment for all?

These words change the dichotomy of what is important. They change the way you feel and you discover you are made up of some wonderfully full emotions and desires. Given priority in your lives these things of importance can become realities in the everyday existence of who you choose to be. Your gift to the world is who you choose to be, everyday. The gift you receive is then in the giving of your true self. Your path is tailored for you, by you. Remember you are the creator of your reality. How you choose to maneuver through it can bring everyday enlightenment. Give more than you get and your love for all will be insurmountable. Long lasting and strong will be your compassion for even those you had contempt for. The miracles of the one true self go beyond anything you can physically see to that of another realm. Be at peace with what I have told you; it is in no way meant to upset or disturb you. My mission here is to teach the children as they appear to you and many times I speak of things foreign to you. Do not let that close your mind to the goodness and the love I have ultimately come to share. Do you hear me when I say be willing to be content, willing to try another way, willing to love? Do you want to live your same trials over and over again? Strive for fulfillment. Strive for unconditional loving my way and then all the other falls away.

Behind every set of eyes is a soul longing to be free. Some are scornful and lashing, others are kind. Be present to whom you a dealing and send love. In recognizing the force that lives within you, you are bringing it up for transformation, for them as well as you. You are sure to have strong feelings when dealt with in a negative way and by working within yourself you change both of you at a deeper level. Your trust in the process is vital and necessary. Just to read this and say OKAY is not enough; you must learn this way of living. Lay before me your self-importance that you might see clearly.

LETTER 128

FIND THE PEACE THAT ELUDES you in my arms. Like a child who has lost their way, you weep, but you can never really be lost, lest you think so in your own mind. My love pours out to you the moment you recognize it is there for you. All is not lost; there is plenty of time to commit yourself to truth. You have wandered long enough in the wilderness of your own hearts. It is time to come to the Father, to come home to the clear, loving path that only I can provide. Your dreams of how life should be cloud the reality of happiness for you. Your constant drive and need to succeed hinder your spiritual path. I am trying to tell each and every one of you to wipe away the fog of man and walk in the clarity of God. Seek to be like your masters who had nothing, yet they were never in want of anything. Their consciousness lied with their God alone and not what man could give them. Their greatest desire was their relationship with the One and that was all. Seek always to do the same.

LETTER 129

TO ALL MY CHILDREN,

I come to communicate to you the last days of Christ. He and his followers together were able to form a relationship deeply bonded by love and respect for one other, able to step forth and change the world. There is nothing wrong with being human, for it is in the integration of the human mind and Christ thinking that all battles are won. I know I must be so careful as to how I speak to you. Do not assume that there are battles that need winning; however, it is in your strength that you combat your mental weaknesses, your physical weaknesses and strengthen your connection with God.

Is this not of the most importance to you? Meld the two as one; combine your physical with the spiritual. Be at peace once and for all. Stay in God consciousness and manifest through your humanness. When Christ spoke to the masses, he did so knowing that one day each person would discover their own oneness with God. The message gave individual power to the people, the power of God, which is and was greater than anything upon the earth. Jesus spoke of a freedom no man could have provided and thus he was killed. For to take the power away from the leaders was heresy and Jesus suffered for it. In doing so he took away much of your pain because he taught a better way of living and being. Your focus has been sadly taken away from your individual power, your true freedom, your direct connection that makes you powerful. Your focus continues to be on the very things that imprison you like your need for importance, your competitiveness, and your hoarding instincts. I come to bring to your mind the way that might bring you peace.

LETTER 130

Your people have suffered long enough and need to know how to escape this suffering. The time has come that to teach will be of the greatest importance. I am choosing those teachers of light now, preparing them, communicating with them their purposes and filling their hearts with the desire to help all of mankind realize, accept and live peacefully, lovingly, and in oneness with me, their Father in heaven. You are no longer destined to be in the darkness of fear and negativity. You are being lifted to the light that you might be whole once again on the physical plane. Form for yourselves a group of great strength that you might support and carry out into the world a light of wisdom and truth. I have been strategically placing around you an arsenal of support that you do not even know exists. You've had your feelings of "I know these people are in my life for a reason" but you know not why. You will know when you ask and follow through with my instruction. Walk slowly at first, getting to know your way on this path of light. As you become more comfortable, draw from those around you extra support and move more quickly and assuredly. Perhaps this is too much to say at this time, but I feel it important to speak to all that have been drawn to these pages.

LETTER 131

FOR A TIME YOUR PEOPLE will cry and mourn the losses of the people who perish in the time to come. For a time the strong feelings of loss will be shared and like a miracle they will all rebound, stronger than before, more vibrant and alive because they will know they are alive because of the death that faces them. At long last your people will understand the need for peace. Instead of talking about it they will be doing something about it. Praise the heavens as each man's heart changes to the good in himself. To express more of what they truly feel inside, to express the divine within them. There is no place for war in this world, but out of war emerges new men with new ambitions and thoughts of how they believe their lives should be lived. More powerful are the aftermaths of war than the missiles that make them. The truth of a people will emerge to shine victorious, to be realized by all for the good of all. Hearts open wide with love for all, for everyone. Treasure the moments with your families, dear ones. Remember to spend time together. Life moves rapidly, children grow and life seems to pass you by. Be present to every moment in your life and make it special.

LETTER 132

LETTER FROM THE MASTERS

*I*T WAS NOT SO VERY long ago that we were among you, living upon the earth for the betterment of man. We have come to you now to share all that we have learned as masters to the world. Our essence is one of pure love and non-judgment. We do not come to accentuate your faults, but to in some way rectify them. Do not harbor defenses against what we have to say; it is only in opening your minds and hearts to us that you begin your peaceful journeys. Satisfied with your present course you seek not the journey of your souls. Delve deep into yourselves to find this purpose for which you've come to be. There is no magic wand or pill that ingested can show you; it is only in losing your will and allowing us access, by faith that we can show you. Ask to be shown, there is so much to do and to follow your heart is the most important of all your tasks. Be free of your worry of how things will turn out. The universe supports you completely when you find your God-given path. How is it we have missed speaking directly to you in the past? Is it because we did not try? No, we have tried. Is it because we did not speak loud enough for you to hear? No, our voices penetrate the heavens. Is it because we lack love for you? Never is there a season that we do not love you completely. We are so near to you.

Be aware that the magic is contained within your heart. By loving all of life and life on earth you become a master yourself. You materialize into someone Christ-like. A beautiful energy that transcends life as you see it now. By leading with your heart instead of your head, you are one with all. The saying "say little, listen much" is coming to mind as we teach you a way of living peacefully with all. Be especially careful not to speak any words in negativity as that creates around you a drain of light energy. Whatever your circumstance is at the moment, make great strides to stay in the positive energy of God light and love. The circumstance passes quickly in this way. If approached with negative energy your heavenly helpers cannot clear the circumstance away. Do not be so skeptical of our presence and divine work in your lives here and now and in the past. The dimensions on which we live are parallel. Many of you have learned to live in both of these dimensions. Bring the higher energy home with you whenever possible and bring the lower energy of earth up to us to be transformed. All of this can be done in prayer. Develop the spiritual habits of prayer and meditation every day. We cannot stress how important that is to spiritual contact. If in your man-driven world there is not fifteen minutes within the whole of twenty-four hours to spend in contact with your Creator, please re-arrange your priorities. It was never the true intention of man to lose such a great and integral part of himself through self-absorption and greed. It was always meant to be a spirit-filled and a spirit-led journey from birth until death. We bless the union of the physical and spiritual and the day the two meet. Rejoice, o child of God. Your spirit comes to you now just in the reading of the words. Halleluiah brethren. Our spirit lives large with you seeking expression and fulfillment. Lift up your eyes towards the heavens that we might gaze upon your beautiful faces. Entrust to God your will and he will entrust his will to you.

O that all the men of earth could hear the message we come to impart. It is rare that we are able to reach the masses but feel the time is neigh. Your feelings have no sustenance in this case it does not matter what you feel. It is the divine and lighted path that will see this task to completion.

Blessings and peace be with you.

LETTER 133

ODAY I SAW THE INTENSITY with which the Masters loved the people. They lived in full Christedness, in that feeling of overwhelming love that you only feel a fraction of. As they spoke to the thousands, love naturally poured forth from their hearts into the crowds. This was why so many followed them. They were pure love, walking, talking and living amongst the people. This is the why, the understanding, of how we are to live. Can you see and visualize how it might have been? How the Masters spoke to the people with so much love and compassion for their darkness, for their heavy hearts. "Yea though I walk through the valley of darkness, I will fear no evil."

The light that shines on the petals of life will come to claim its beloved ones. The understanding will be clear that those who have stood fast upon the unshakable rock will glorify me in heaven because of their unending faith in me, God the Father, the never ending one of all. Blessed indeed are the ones who see, who know and who feel. They have chosen the God of their understanding and made it their life's passion to communicate with him daily by hour and by minute. In their enlightened states there is no separation between God and man no more than there be separation between Father and Son. Do you see the difference between a follower and one who is lost? It is of great importance to bring those who are lost home into the fold. You cannot sit by as enlightened ones and allow your brothers to flounder in the dark. To risk being thought a fool is no risk when a man's life is at hand. Share with them your knowledge of others who were lost in a tangle of worldly elements, but who now live freely in the knowledge and clarity that only the Holy Spirit can give. The man who takes on this mission in his life is of great wisdom and knowledge. Allow my angels to work through each of you for the highest good of all mankind. Person to person, heart to heart, soul to soul lift your own collective thoughts to a higher realm through communication with the Father. How can you live a life in which you have no daily instruction? Let you learn day by day from the Creator what we must do to co-create lives worth living.

Pray and meditate on this daily that I may give you instructions on what to do next.

Practice, practice, practice . . . fine tune your communications with the angels and Holy Spirit. Strengthen your gifts and therefore strengthen your confidence. You are 100% supported in this.

Be patient. Events will come as you are guided. Begin to study the words I have spoken here so that you might one day teach.

LETTER 134

I WILL NOT TELL YOU THE why's and the many in's and out's of the universe in which you live, but I will with ease tell you the meanings of your lives. Each one has a purpose to fulfill upon the earth just as you do in heaven. It is in your connection to me, the light being of oneness, that you discover yours. It is all based in love; every soul purpose begins with love. Although you would have me tell you yours is to save the world it is not. It is to loosen yourselves from the hold of the world, lose ego, find love in every situation, and live joyfully because of it. Because of this transformation within yourselves you will be able to do all things. Be free in your choices because you are no longer attached to the physical. By focusing fully on love, you have far surpassed anything the physical world could give you. You have tapped into the never-ending source of everything.

Can you understand? You of yourselves have created nothing nor will you of yourselves create anything in the future. With God's inspiration and will you can co-create anything. The more focus and energy you can devote to love, the more powerful you become in controlling matter and your own lives. And the more in control you become of all circumstances around you.

Believe that the source of all, living and creating through you, can give you all that you seek which is peace, happiness, and joyful living. Believe, dear ones of this world, that this is a place that can be obtained by all, starting with the smallest, yet the largest of steps . . . love for one another, complete and unconditional. Conditional love has never been taught, so why are your religious entities doing it now? If they so loved the world as the Masters did there would be no ill will or negativity spewed on anyone, regardless of religious background or otherwise. If you want to speak out to the nations of the world and make that difference your soul keeps nudging you to make, start within your own household. Begin in your communities and begin with love. Greatness comes to those who love all. Serve the world well. It is your greatest mission in life.

Never be afraid. There is no fear where love reigns supreme, no matter what the outer may show you. With love at the core of all things, fear and horror dissipate. Be of one mind, children, and of one hope. That of eternal light and peace so that all can be brethren under one Holy God. Symbolism of this great task will be the beginning of understanding. Where languages will always have their limitations, symbolism will transcend all barriers and bring understanding to all. ⨍ will stand for God light, the one God over all. No separate names, no separate ideals, the same to all. Do you see where I lead you? To one universal understanding of the whole. There will be no place for separateness in the age to come. You will alleviate the world of its difference in thinking. Every nation and every culture has a world of its own understanding. Step by step we create one world through shared perspectives and symbolism. What we share we cannot destroy. Shared hope and shared understanding.

LETTER 135

WHEN YOU ARE ALONE WE know the graciousness that has been given to us through Christ. For when you are alone your errors magnify to a deafening sound that you cannot, nor should, ignore. There, with all the life of a thousand men, they spring forth with renewed judgment of which you will either crumble beneath the weight or rise victorious with the knowing that your God is a most loving God and my intention for you is nothing but the holiest, most joyful existence possible. Where are your sacred brethren now, but in heaven watching over you, instructing and leading you to the pathways of peace. Is it not on this path that you will find much joy? Pray they guide you to discover the beauty that lies within yourselves. I do not ask that your lives be laid down, only your human (ego) side so full of ambition and conflict. I repeat myself because it is such a part of you, difficult to remove. If it had been done I would not insist on saying so over again. I bless the holy ground upon which you walk. Recognize it as such and begin to walk with holy confidence. How long must I wait for you to see that it is I, the Father, that calls you and it is I, the Father, that will care for you within the will? It is your heart's utmost desire to follow me unto the ends of the earth knowing your bliss lies there.

Jesus walked on the earth so that you would know how to live. To live without doubt, fear and disbelief. He came to show you, as the example, how to live and breathe with a oneness that transcends all. To take note of his life is not enough. You must take the steps to integrate it into your lives. Because you were of human flesh and unable to accept his divine example, you as a race have taken it upon yourselves to interpret his life in a way you could understand. Blessed be the believers, but I say to you, you have gone astray in your ideas and idioms. Place your ears to heaven and hear the true life that Christ lived. To follow in his footsteps should be the greatest desire among men, not to gain more power or miracles, but to live in complete harmony and peace. Do you know what that feels like? Remotely? Do you know what it means? That peace where you know you are in heaven yet your feet are on the earthly ground. The place of in between, where you live amongst men yet commune with the Spirit. The joy, the release, the freedom that this way of living brings is for all men, not the privileged few. Because you were made in the image of me, the all of everything, your soul knows no peace until it is reunited with the all of everything, me. Why do you keep yourselves from it, running in the opposite direction, getting yourselves deeper into conflict and disharmony? It will not be until you surrender that your freedom comes. The Satan that destroys you is real within your own being. I am here to reveal what you already know. Is it out there in the world looking to destroy you? No, it is within you because you have allowed it to reside there. You have taken on a very human belief that it is a force against you, too strong to overcome, that will always be pursuing you. Half of this is true. It is a force to be reckoned with and you cannot rid yourself of it without the Spirit of God, but it is not a true threat that is outside of you. It is one of your own making which you have allowed to take up residence with you. Many call it ego, that voice within that brings about doubt and fear. I come to release you from this way of thinking (this demon) so that you may conquer within you the greatest doubts and fears by bringing light to the darkness that resides there.

Why now, at this time, have I come to explain? For too many years you have misinterpreted my words. Speaking truth, The Christ was never speaking from a human self, but from a man on earth whose heart and soul were completely one with God. After his death and resurrection the truth that was spoken through man was not pure, but that of heaven filtered through the mind of man. Just as I speak to you now, my truth is filtered through the human mind, more purely than before because of the higher vibrations upon the earth now. To take a man's words as face value is to be without wisdom. Question all of life and the meaning of all. Your perception may not be right for everyone, but allow yourself power to discern for yourself. To be pleasing unto me you must take action with in your own life to assure yourself of the truth that lies within the Spirit and soul within you. To be haphazardly thrown about upon the waves of life is to be without sense of true self. Anchor your vessel in the word I speak to you. Know that you have a choice; you have abilities beyond your comprehension. Awaken, o children of God, and see your strengths. See how the Father wants you to live. Blissfully in right choices that come from right thinking, which come from God. To be in the constant beautiful presence of God is my dream. The ability to do so is your reality. Come into my arms all you nations of earth and be blessed with true understanding and hope for your people. I see within my heart a world of prosperity where every person is touched by the heavens and each person knows why he came to be on the earth. To shine God light to their brethren, their country, their world. Embrace me into your lives that I might embrace you completely. Your future does not lie with hatred nor abuse of one another. As you evolve and mature you will no longer accept this within your world and will seek to rid your world of the negativity. Now do not misconstrue these words to think killing and annihilation is all right; it is not. For if you are truly living from a higher place you will only seek to pray for the lost and love them. It is not the duty of patrons to forcefully impose their opinions upon others. Be at peace. Be at peace, for love does conquer all. Send love throughout your world and you will be blessed with love throughout your own life. Be assured I come not to preach of a better way, but a different way that is available to you now. The way is already here to be recognized by all. Forgive the perceived wrongs of others and hold yourself accountable for doing so. Forgiveness of self cannot occur until you have done so with others. Be of good heart and allow no one to tear you from your position among the heavens. Your place of peace greatly depends upon your reactions to others.

Greet me each day with a renewed commitment to peace within yourself that you might live wholly in that place of understanding and revelation. Not only for yourself, but also for the world around you. My children, you are the hope of humanity. You are the light of the world. You will bring about the dream of peace and the reality of oneness. You will not stand by in idle contemplation of what is, but will resolve yourselves to be the ones that change it.

All is complete and I am done.

AFTERWARD

*N*OW, TWO YEARS LATER, I sit surrounded by fields of green; the river slowly but steadily flows by. My life is beautiful here in the mountains.

I am remembering the past four years of my life since these writings began. Remembering and knowing all at the same time how my life has changed. The miracles keep coming and I am filled with awe and gratitude for every step I've been shown and every step I've been given the courage to take.

It was June 28, 2002, when all of this began for me. When it seemed like my life began. Until that moment I could never clear the fog that surrounded me. I had never heard, felt, or even imagined the voice of God. But somehow, on this day in June 2002, I opened up to a presence, a force, a loving constant. I opened up to the voice of God that said, "Go and write." And now I say to you "Go write," that we might all have a clearer vision of who we are. For as God so eloquently put it,

> We are the Hope of Humanity
> We are the Light of the World
> We Bring about the Dream of Peace and the Reality of Oneness
> We Do Not Stand by in Idle Contemplation of What Is
> But Resolve Ourselves to Be the Ones that Change It

For more information on *How to Hear the Voice of God* workshops and retreats, one on one consultations with Karen, and other related services, call

1 800 970 3848

Or visit

www.karencoffey.com
or
www.hopeofhumanity.org